HOW TO LOVE

A

BROKEN MAN

WRITTEN BY:

MyKisha Mac

Contains explicit language & adult themes
suitable for ages 16+

Other Novels Written by MyKisha Mac:

The Love of a Good Man

Introducing Star IV

Hate That I Love You 1 2 & 3

Sky & Sincere: His Rider, Her Roller 1 2 & 3

Chase & Kassidy: All Eyes On Us

My Best Friend's Brother: The Ultimate
Betrayal

~

Coming Soon:
TBD

Follow MyKisha Mac on Social Media

Facebook: The MyKisha Mac Experience

https://www.facebook.com/TheMykishaMac Experience/

Please feel free to like the page.

Website: www.mykishamac.com **Please subscribe to mailing list to stay in the loop, get first dabs on sneak peeks, and chances to win FREE copies.**

Reading Group, A New Chapter:

https://www.facebook.com/groups/anewchapter.my

kishamacreaders A NEW CHAPTER

A New Chapter Publications:

https://www.facebook.com/anewchapterpub/

Blog:

www.mykishamac4book.wordpress.com

Email: mykishamac@gmail.com

Twitter: @lovejones007

IG@mykisha.mac

TEXT ANEWCHAPTER

at 22828

TO JOIN MAILING LIST

DEDICATION

I thank my readers for riding with me through my writing career and those who have congratulated and wished me well as I start *A New Chapter* in my life with my publishing company A NEW CHAPTER PUBLICATIONS. Your well wishes and kind words are appreciated. Just as I've given you my best with my books, I plan to continue to work hard by producing quality books from the Authors of ANCP.

Be on the lookout for some creative banging books to come!

I thank my family and friends who continue to support me through it all. My special gifts from heaven, Di'Jionae and Tank; mommy loves you forever.

To my readers—you all are AMAZING! I can't thank you enough. Without you, there is no MyKisha Mac. I appreciate your support and connections via social media. It gives my heart great joy when you tell me that you really enjoyed a story written by me, and ask for more books by me.

Wow… as a writer, that's the most crucial words to ever hear, and it motivates me to keep doing what I do to give you the entertainment you deserve. Thanks for welcoming me into your homes, whether it's from an eReader or a paperback. I sincerely thank you!

As a friend, I am so glad that you are a part of my life. I take into consideration what you expect from me, and I appreciate the time you take to tell me in reviews. I think about you all often, and how may I bring you stories that will warm your hearts, piss you off (lol), make you laugh, make you cry and encourage you if possible in any way that I can from the stories I write.

Forever grateful to each and every one of you!

With all of my love,

MyKisha Mac

"It is easier to build strong children than to repair broken men."

~ Fredrick Douglas

"If a piece of knotted string can unleash the wind and if a drowned man can awaken... then I believe a broken man can heal."

~ Annie Proulx

"Just as a puzzle can be put back together, piece by piece, so can a broken man.

~ MyKisha Mac

Love doesn't have to be picture-perfect, it should be genuine and shot straight from the heart. If we all search deep within ourselves, we would realize that we are more alike than we are different. We'd grasp the notion that we all want the same thing in this life; REAL LOVE.

It doesn't matter if the whole world is against us or not; if we have that one special person who is willing to stand on the front line with us, no matter what, we would know that we would be okay, no matter the outcome.

Someone who won't bail when the going gets tough, but instead, equip themselves with armor and be ready to go to war with us at a drop of a dime. Someone who would be there; not only in the times of goodness and peace, but also in the times of strife and adversity.

Those are the times that matters the most anyways.

If we are honest with ourselves, we'd realize that we all want that special someone who has our back; right or wrong, good or bad, but also who's not afraid to take a stand and tell us when we are wrong.

Someone who doesn't comfort our feelings and emotions with a beautiful lie. Someone who is able and willing to volunteer the ugly truth, because they know no matter how bad it may be, they'll still stand right by our side.

They say love is a battlefield. Most of us walk around with the scars and wounds to prove it. Only the strong survive, and only the brave accept the challenges that true love brings.

Chapter One
The Wrath of the Arch Bishop

"You, nor the bastard that you are carrying are no longer welcomed into my home! I can't even stand to look at you right now! Get out and get out now!" thundered from Bishop's mouth.

Bishop's tone was stern as usual, and he felt no remorse whatsoever for his outrage in spoken words. Satin had done the unthinkable as a preacher's kid. The saints were watching, and they were ready to condemn at the drop of a dime.

The Alexanders' moved from Jackson, Mississippi to Henderson, Nevada when Satin was only the tender age of two. Arch Bishop, who wholeheartedly believed he could change a society that was filled with sin in the city, didn't realize that his own daughter would become a part of the baby momma club. Bishop knew Las Vegas wouldn't be a walk in the park, but he never saw the day coming that his own precious daughter would soon make the mistakes of so many other young black females her age.

Bishop found out his beloved Satin, who he raised in the church, was pregnant with a child, and it was unacceptable to his biblical teachings that a young unmarried girl should have sexual relations with anyone. Bishop was publicly embarrassed and could no longer stand to even be in the same room as Satin. She had tarnished the Alexanders good wholesome name that he worked so hard to obtain in a city that believed that what happened in Vegas stayed in Vegas. That saying was the total opposite of Bishop's Southern roots and upbringing.

Bishop was blinded by Satin's shyness as a child, the southern traditional behavior that was taught by him, and a well-groomed personality that Satin also possessed in her young adulthood. Bishop felt the need to hound Satin about staying away from boys until she was considered ready for one in his eyes. Satin appeared to have no interest in boys whatsoever, until a boy by the name of Nolan joined the church.

Through her father's eyes, Satin became tainted, drowned in sin and was no longer the precious little girl with smooth chestnut skin and sleek curly hair, that he laid eyes on when she came out of her mother's womb. To Bishop's surprise, the same sinful world he tried to protect Satin from had gotten to her, and there was nothing he could do about it. Bishop's grip was so tight around Satin that the first chance she got to spend alone with a boy to spread her wings, she forgot what was instilled in her from birth. She lost all self-control. Satin had spread more than her wings that late evening, she became pregnant the exact same night she lost her virginity.

Nolan was also a member of the church, but wasn't raised by a father who was a pastor. He viewed things a bit different, and was more drawn to the streets than church, which his mother forced him to attend.

Nolan was rough around the edges, causing his single mother pure hell, and Satin was immediately smitten by him. Nolan was far different from the other boys in the church. He didn't follow the rules and didn't feel guilty about it at all. Satin thought of Nolan as being courageous and not afraid to be who God made him to be. All the other boys of the church respected Bishop, but Nolan gave him a run for his money. Bishop even advised his mother to take him to the church counselor because he sensed that Nolan had suppressed anger at his father, who had abandoned him and his mother. Bishop believed that was the underlining cause of Nolan's bad behavior.

Bishop pastored a well-respected congregation. The church trusted him and looked to Bishop for spiritual guidance. He was infused and deep rooted with down south biblical teachings; thanks to his father, who was also a pastor. Bishop taught strictly by the book; the Holy bible that was, and lived by every word he taught, but somehow, forgiveness slipped through the cracks and wasn't one of his strong suits. Bishop allowed his anger to overshadow his heart that was filled with God's holy word and divine love. Somewhere down the line, he involuntarily allowed it to become a heart of stone towards his own daughter.

The Alexanders were religious people and didn't have room in their lives for human error; at least, Bishop thought so anyway. He had an image to uphold and a congregation to lead. Bishop started to think how he, as the Lord's Shepard, could lead a flock of sheep when his own home was out of order and in chaos.

Bishop told Satin that he couldn't house a harlot, who was also carrying a bastard child in her womb. Satin was devastated and filled with grief. The same father she grew up to love and respect had turned his back on her. Satin was forced to leave her comfort zone and fend for herself.

*****

"Nah, that's enough, Bishop! I done had 'bout enough of you condemning this girl. For heaven's sake, she's your daughter; our daughter! If God can forgive us for our transgressions, then so can we forgive others! Are we even reading from the same bible, because I don't recall ever reading anything about not forgiving our own children? This is not of God's doing, Arch Bishop Alexander, this is all you!" Carolyn argued as she walked towards her daughter, Satin, and tried to comfort her as she shielded her from her stern husband, Arch Bishop Alexander's, who demanded to be referred to be referred to as just Bishop, wrath.

When Carolyn called Bishop by his entire name, he knew that she was upset with him. Carolyn was what Christians refer to as a meek woman. She held Bishop in the highest regards and very seldom, if ever, went against his better judgements.

"Woman, don't you dare question my faith! Who in the HELL do you think you are speaking to! You have been warned and I won't say it again!" Bishop tightened his lips and raised his eyebrows as wrinkles appeared in his forehead.

Oh, that's right, O holy one. You are the Arch Bishop, one of God's most faithful servants, according to your parents who named you as such. Thanks for *ALWAYS reminding us all. Who in the hell names their child that anyway? Surely not sane black folk,* Carolyn thought to herself in anger for a moment as she did what Bishop demanded and lowered her tone.

Carolyn never defied her husband, she always respected Bishop and what he said, but that day, he had gone way too far. Bishop was throwing their daughter out on the street and had no regard as to how it would affect her in the future. Bishop was so consumed with hurt and anger, he couldn't see Satin for who she really was, his beloved daughter.

"All I'm saying is, our daughter made a mistake; she's human, Bishop. We all have fallen short of God's glory at some point in our lives, haven't we? Satin just made a simple mistake, that's it."

"There's nothing simple about having sex before marriage, Carolyn, when she KNEW better. There's nothing simple about bringing a child into this world as a bastard, and most importantly, there's nothing simple about sinning against God!" Bishop spat as he put on his holier than thou armor.

"Please Bishop, please don't do this! Don't do this to our daughter!" Carolyn pleaded with an earnest heart. "Where will she go; she's only seventeen. How can you just throw Satin out there on the street to fend for herself? How could you?!" Carolyn continued to beg as tears began to saturate her high cheek bones.

Carolyn was a spitting image of Diahann Carroll. She exuded massive beauty and pure grace just as the African American actress, who was a pure Goddess. Carolyn was well respected by her family and close friends; she was the glue that kept the Alexander family together.

Although, Carolyn always worked her magic from behind the scenes, allowing her husband to lead as she followed, Carolyn was a woman of opinion, and Bishop knew she would buckle down, but had to voice her opinion first.

Satin was fearful of her father, always were, even as a little child. Not fearful in a way that made it seem as if she was frightened by Bishop, Satin highly respected him and never wanted to disappoint Daddy. Bishop had a thunder to his tone, and when he spoke, it was as if God himself had spoken.

Satin wouldn't dare to even dream about rising up to Arch Bishop Alexander. She knew she made a terrible mistake, but what Satin didn't know was that, it would cause her to lose a place in her home; more importantly, her father's respect. Bishop was hugely disappointed in Satin and the promiscuous choices she made.

"I'm done talking and I mean what I say!" Bishop gawked at Satin. "Believe me, this hurts me way more than it hurts you. I warned you about the troubled boy when I saw the two of you chatting in bible study, but you wouldn't listen. Now look what you've brought on yourself, and the shame you've brought to this family."

Bishop stormed out of the family room and went into his study. He prayed to God and began to read the bible. Bishop's heart was shattered that his baby girl had gotten herself pregnant and was only seventeen and unmarried. Bishop believed in his heart that he was doing the right thing. He believed Satin had to somehow accept and learn from her mistakes, and the only way to do that was without his help, and with tough love.

Bishop believed that only God could ultimately teach his daughter the lesson that was to be taught. Providing cushion for Satin's fall was not a way for her to learn life lessons according to him, and it was the way Bishop's parents had taught him. Carolyn, on the other hand, felt nothing but compassion for their daughter. Carolyn continued to comfort Satin.

"I'm so sorry, baby. I wish things could be different; Momma really does. I wish your father would accept that times have changed since when we were growing up."

Satin looked at Carolyn, but she couldn't offer up a response in that moment. She was trying to digest the fact that she would become a young unmarried mother.

Carolyn continued, "You know how your father gets. As I've said many times before, lets allow Bishop time to sleep on it, and I'm sure he'll change his mind by tomorrow. It takes him a little longer to process things, unlike myself. When problems arise, I'm already looking for a solution. I don't dwell on things, unlike your father does. I deal with them head on and move on."

Satin took in her mother's words. She tried her damndest to process as much as she could with everything that was going on that day. She was beyond overwhelmed and didn't have a clue as to what she would have to face out in a world all on her own.

"It's okay, Momma. He's right, Bishop is right." Satin took a deep breath and then continued, "I made my own bed hard, and now I must lay in it," Satin spoke full of guilt.

"Don't say that, Satin. You made a mistake, a mistake… we all make them. And besides, the last time I checked, children were a gift from God, no matter how they are conceived," Carolyn whispered as she softly placed her hand on the side of Satins wet face.

"That may be true Momma, but this will change my life forever. You and I both know that and so does Bishop. I'm seventeen, only seventeeeeen…." Satin begun to cry again. "Please Momma, don't let him do this to me. I have nowhere else to go. Pleaseeee let me stay," Satin pleaded in fear of what was waiting for her beyond the comfort of her home.

"It's okay baby, it's okay; everything will be okay, I promise," Carolyn spoke as she took her broken daughter into her bosom and clasped Satin tightly.

Carolyn wiped Satin's dreary eyes, and rubbed the back of her head. It killed Carolyn to watch Satin fall apart right before her very own eyes. Carolyn knew there was no way Satin could possible go through being seventeen, pregnant and homeless all on her own.

"Listen to me," Carolyn placed her hands on each side of Satin's fragile shoulders, and stared genuinely into her drowning eyes. "No, I don't agree with the choice that you've made, but I forgive you, just as the lord has forgiven me for all of my sins, and I will do all that I can to help you get through this," Carolyn assured Satin as she reached on the table and snatched her purse. "Here… this is two hundred dollars." She put the money inside of Satin's hand. "Go check into a hotel tonight, and it's as I've said, Bishop will sleep on it, and I'm quite sure he will forgive you, just as I have, and allow you to come back home. This is your home, baby; you belong here with your family. I just wish there's was more I could do. Just bear with me, and give me some time. I'll work on it, I will. I will fix this."

Carolyn's heart sunk as she shared the feelings of helplessness and spiritually wounded with Satin. Carolyn's one and only child was in a tough place and neither of them had the head of their household, Bishop's support.

Carolyn knew her husband better than anyone. If Bishop said something, he very well meant it, and there was no way in hell that he would go back on his words. Bishop was stubborn, straight forward, and cut no corners with anyone; not even his own family.

Satin found a way to pull herself together for a brief moment. She took a deep breath and slowly let it out. "Thanks Momma, I don't know what I would do without you," Satin cried as she tightly hugged Carolyn as she searched for strength to help her get through what she had to face.

"I pray to God that you won't ever have to find out, baby," Carolyn assured her as she clasped Satin's back tightly once more, and her compassionate lips brushed against Satin's forehead.

Carolyn walked Satin to the bedroom in efforts to comfort Satin in her moment of despair. Satin packed a duffel bag before cuddling with Carolyn, she held on to the comfort of her mother's bosom and scent as though it may have been the last time. A heavy-hearted Carolyn walked her daughter to the front door. After their sad goodbyes, Satin jumped into the red Kia Soul her parents gifted her for her sweet sixteen. She drove from Henderson, Nevada to Las Vegas and checked herself into a cheap motel, not too far from the Vegas strip.

"Damn you, Satan! I will *not* let you destroy my family!" Carolyn dropped to her knees and wept.

Chapter Two
How Could I Throw Away a Miracle

Satin Alexander had dug a hole so deep for herself, she had to go through hell and high waters to try and climb out of it. Being a P.K, Preacher's Kid, had its perks, but also had its downfalls. The judgement by the world was tough, but the judgement by her father was a lot tougher. Satin's holier than thou father found it harder to forgive her when she sinned, than when others sinned because a P. K. should know better, right? They were equipped with the word of God, and had examples by the home life to follow.

After nine months of agony and despair, Satin gave birth to a healthy beautiful baby boy on New Year's Day. It was just as her mother had told her, children were a gift from God, no matter how they were conceived. Although Satin had steered away from

God for a moment, she still believed in His promise and principles. She asked God for forgiveness, but also thanked him for one of his greatest gifts; the gift of life in her precious son.

Satin didn't know what she would name her new bundle of joy until she realized that, after the storm, came a beautiful rainbow. She decided to name her baby Noah, Noah Alexander. It was close to the baby's father's name Nolan, and was a reminder to herself that God still loved her no matter what her sins were, and that He always kept his promises just as he did with Noah of the bible.

Although Satin landed herself a temporary spot on the sidewalk of the Vegas strip, she was currently living in a women's shelter for single mothers. But that day, no matter what Satin's situation was, her heart was full of joy. She took one look at Noah and knew God had plans for his life and hers as well.

Satin never thought of Noah as a mistake, she believed he was her blessing. Her promise from God, and naming him Noah, as in the great Noah of the bible, would remind her of God's promises every time she looked at him. Baby Noah was Satin's forbidden rainbow, and there was nothing in the world she wouldn't do for him.

Satin was in love. A new kind of love; one that she never dreamed even existed. Noah became her reason for living, and her reason for wanting nothing but the best for her and her son. It wasn't easy for Satin, not by any means, but she pushed through anyway without any help from her father, and limited help from her mother. Not because Carolyn didn't want to help her daughter financially as promised, but because Carolyn didn't have her own source of income coming in, and taking money out of the joint account she shared with Bishop only raised his suspicions.

Bishop meant what he said, he wanted nothing to do with Satin nor her child that he referred to as a bastard. Carolyn kept the peace in her home. That's what any good God fearing wife would do if anyone asked her. Honoring her husband was Carolyn's way of honoring God, even if she didn't agree with him. Carolyn, the virtuous God fearing woman wasn't in the business of dishonoring God.

Carolyn would visit Satin and her grandson at the shelter and bring them food and toys for Noah when she could. She did it behind her husband's back, but just couldn't sat back and do nothing at all.

Nolan, Noah's father, contributed very little. He was young, not focused, and was into other girls. Nolan wasn't ready to be a dad by any means. He was only eighteen himself when Satin became pregnant. Once Satin told Nolan she was pregnant, Nolan vanished without a trace, and stopped answering Satin's calls until the day Noah was born. Nolan decided to show up at the hospital with a bag of pampers and a car seat that his mother had gotten for his baby.

Satin forgave Nolan for abandoning her when she needed him the most. She decided to forgive Nolan because she believed it was the right thing to do for her son, and she didn't want to be another statistic; a young black single mother. Satin wanted baby Noah to see and know who his daddy was and where he came from.

Noah was a spitting image of his father, and once Nolan realized that, he started to help Satin out more, but still refused to give up his bad boy ways. He figured he could do both; be a father to his son and still a lady's man. Satin just didn't have any idea that he was, and she would soon learn, she couldn't raise a man, nor could she teach him how to be a father to his very own son.

Chapter Three
When I Say, I do, I Will

Three Years Later....

Flames flickered across the room as vibrant white candles illuminated the Cathedral. Sebastian Smith, stood handsomely groomed in front of an anxious crowd, drenched in more love than he could mentally process. He waited for his bride to be to mysteriously trail down the aisle of soft rosy petals in a beautiful white dress that he believed was made perfectly, just for her.

The bridesmaids and groomsmen began to trail the pasty carpet as the flower girl and ring bearer continued to shower the runner with silk like emblems. The priest came out and stood before the podium, with a serious glare plastered on his flushed face. He peered over at Sebastian for a second, and offered a subtle grin as his eyes then began to make their way around the exquisite decorated

Cathedral; taking in yet, another beautiful moment when two people would come together in a covenant before God.

Sebastian's heart raced a mile a minute, perspiration crept underneath his armpits, as his stomach stiffened in knots. He was full of excitement that the day had finally come, that he would marry Angela; the love of his life, the apple of his eyes, the woman he believed God had blessed him with. The only woman Sebastian had ever dreamed of spending the rest of his life with until death would do them part. Angela was special to Sebastian; he believed God created her especially for him.

The happy young couple had strategically planned for months, and was prepared to give their audience a reflection of their devoted love to one another. The clock ticked and the house of worship was pleasantly quiet. The organ player played angelic melodies that perfected the moment and soothed the entire room. Any and everyone who was in attendance felt like they were in for a beautiful surprise; a moment to remember.

After a couple of melodies, and the wedding party finally standing in their appointed places came the popular tune, 'Here Comes the Bride'. Everyone stood to their feet, and feasted their eyes to the entrance of the Cathedral, eagerly awaiting Angela to grace them with an extravagant entrance. The organist continued to play instrumental delights as the doorway to the opening of the room was empty. Heads begin to turn and mouths began to whisper.

Sebastian kept his cool because he knew without a shadow of doubt that Angela loved him more than life itself, and he'd already helped to pay for a wedding of a lifetime; just as his bride to be had wanted. Everything was perfect if you'd asked him.

Sebastian hunched his shoulders, inhaled deeply and released slowly, but kept his engrossed eyes at the opening of the doorway as he awaited his beautiful wife to be.

Finally came a silhouette of a physique, but to Sebastian's dismay, it wasn't the love of his life, the apple of his eyes, the woman he believed God has blessed him with. It was the father of the bride with a message to the audience and to him.

Jim, Angela's father, cleared his throat as he began to try and utter some kind of explanation as to why it was him standing in the entrance, instead of his daughter the bride to be.

"Umm... first off, I would like to apologize for this unfortunate delay, and without any further ado... Angela has a message for all of you. She wanted nothing more but to relay it herself, but uh... she's having a really difficult time gathering herself to be able to stand here and somehow face all of you."

The audience gasped in total disbelief. Sebastian's almond perfect eyes enlarged, as his thick dark eyebrows raised to his temple. Not seeing his bride to be walk down the aisle ready to marry him, but instead her father to relay a message, made Sebastian's heart sunk into his stomach as a lump formed in his throat.

Jim took in a long deep breath and continued to speak as he stood with his long arms at his waist's side. "I'm sorry folks, but there will *not* be a wedding here today. On behalf of my daughter Angela, myself and my wife, we are very sorry for any inconvenience this may have caused you."

Jim paused for a brief second as his eyes traveled towards Sebastian. The look of terror was written all over Sebastian's face. He could not prepare himself for what Jim wanted to say to him.

"Sebastian…" Jim continued, but before he could address him, Sebastian took off running to the stairway of the church, and straight up to the bride's dressing room.

There was a sign on the door that read *The Bride's Chamber Do Not Disturb*. Sebastian ignored the sign and opened the door. He found Angela in her wedding dress, sitting in a chair with swollen eyes and running mascara as if she'd been balling her eyes out all night long.

"Angie, baby, what's wrong? Why are you crying? Talk to me baby," Sebastian asked full of worry.

Angela reached for a Kleenex that was placed on the vanity desk. Her mother stood outside the door, knocking to come in, but Sebastian and Angela both ignored the knocks. They had other things to worry about rather than who was on the other side of the door dying to get in. Their wedding was not happening, and Sebastian was in desperate need of answers as to why.

Angela's mother turned the knob and let herself in anyway.

"Mom, pleaseee… give us a few minutes," Angela pleaded as she dabbed her running eyes and smeared eyeliner; removing one of her false lashes. "I need to…."

Angela's mother cut her off. "Honey, are you okay? What's going on and what are you carrying on about? Today is supposed to be one of the happiest days of your life! Pull yourself together, and let's go get married!" Mrs. Winfield demanded.

"Mom, pleaseeee…" Angela pleaded again with tears still pouring from her eyes, loosening the glue of the other eyelash as it fell off too. "You don't understand, you never do, and that's why I spoke to Daddy about it. Please, let Daddy fill you in because I really need to speak to Sebastian," Angela cried as she removed the fallen lash from her face and placed it in the tissue.

Sebastian stood before his wife to be and couldn't believe what was happening. He led himself to believe they were happy, and they both were equally excited to become husband and wife. Sebastian had seen Angela a day before the wedding, and she appeared to be a little down, but far more than fine. When Sebastian asked Angela, what was wrong, she told her future husband that she was overwhelmed by the planning, but was okay and couldn't wait to be his wife. Sebastian dismissed his worry, and guaranteed Angela that everything would be okay. He told her that they only had one more day to get through, and after would finally relax on their honeymoon as husband and wife.

Sebastian convinced Angela that the hard part was behind them, which was planning the wedding to make sure that everything was perfect, as she wanted it to be. Angela seemed to be okay after the talk with Sebastian and they later departed.

"But honey…" Angela's mom continued to push with a worried expression plastered on her perfectly made-up face.

"Mrs. Winfield, it's okay; I'll take care of it. I think Angie's just a bit overwhelmed with all the planning and everything. Please, give us a few minutes, and I'm sure everything will be okay," Sebastian assured the older woman as he escorted Angela's mom to the door, but deep down inside, he was unsure of everything himself.

Sebastian gave Mrs. Winfield a counterfeit smile as he tried to convince his future mother in law and himself that everything was fine between him and Angela.

"Okay, I'll give you all some time. Please take care of it, Sebastian. There's plenty of people here waiting for a wedding to happen and so am I," Mrs. Winfield sincerely expressed as she softly placed her hand on the side of Sebastian face.

Mrs. Winfield was very fond of her son in law to be, and believed Sebastian was the perfect man for her daughter. Far better than the controlling, possessive boyfriend Angela had before him, and Angela's mother wanted nothing more than to see her end up married to a guy like Sebastian.

"I know… and I will," Sebastian assured Mrs. Winfield again as he escorted her out of the room and locked the door behind her so he and Angela could finally talk.

Sebastian walked back towards Angela sitting in the chair, still sobbing and stooped down before her. "Angie what's wrong, love? Don't let the stress of planning everything ruin your special day; our special day. Just try and relax for a minute and take in a deep breath. Everything will be okay. You have been waiting on this day for months and it's finally here. Let's seize the moment, love. Forget everything else, forget that there's people waiting. This is our day baby; yours and mine. What are we doing in here even talking about this? Let's go get married," Sebastian insisted.

Angela wiped her face with a fresh tissue and gazed deeply into Sebastian's eyes as he stared intensely back at her. "Sebastian…." Angela mouthed as she took in a deep breath, and slowly exhaled and continued, "I can't do this. I've been trying to convince myself to go through with this wedding for months now, but I realize that I can't do this, I just can't."

Sebastian stood to his feet and took a couple of steps back. He loosened his black bowtie around his neck as it felt as though his breath was sucked out of his Adam's apple. He placed one hand on his hip, and the other on his for head. Sebastian thought to himself for a brief second before he could give Angela a response.

"What exactly is that supposed to mean, Angela? What do you mean you've been trying to convince yourself to marry me for months now? What…You don't love me anymore so you have to somehow *convince* yourself to marry me?" Sebastian asked with eyes of fiery and a heart that was slowly breaking into a million pieces.

Angela stood to her feet. "That's not what I said, Sebastian, but I don't know. I do love you, but I now know that I'm not *in* love with you. It wouldn't be fair to you to marry a woman who's not ready to love you like a wife should love her husband. I have so many things in my life that I want to do, and I'm sorry, but those things are not things that a wife should be doing. I'm so sorry…"

Sebastian swiftly turned his back on Angela and dropped his chin into his chiseled chest. He couldn't believe the words that rolled off Angela's tongue. His pride was shattered and heart crushed. Sebastian believed he and Angela were on the same page, and had made plans to build a life together. Suddenly, Angela's words and actions just didn't add up, and didn't make any sense. Sebastian thought there had to be more to what Angela told him, and he wanted answers; he needed answers.

Sebastian slowly turned back around. He pierced Angela's eyes with his own. He silenced his anger, and tried his damndest to remain calm. "What kind of things, Angela? What kind of things do you feel you need to do that a wife cannot do? Explain that one to me, pleaseeee, because I'm confused like a motherfucker right about now." Sebastian's grave tone resonated through the room.

"Plenty of things, Sebastian, I don't know. I'm just freshly out of medical school and haven't even began to start really living my life yet on my own. I believe there's just some things I need to experience on my own, before I can even begin to experience with someone else."

"And you just coming to this conclusion NOW! This is BULLSHIT MAN and you know it! What's the real reason, huh? What's the real reason you feel like you don't want to marry me instead of the bullshit you trying to sell me? Is it someone else? Are you in love with another man because you surely, obviously, you don't give a fuck about me?"

Angela dropped her head in her chest. She couldn't even continue to look Sebastian into his eyes.

"You know what, your quietness speaks volumes," Sebastian said as he walked toward the door.

"How could you do this shit to me? After EVERYTHING that I've done for you! How could you betray me in this way, Angie? How could you, man?"

Angela's dad heard Sebastian's bark through the upstairs door. He attempted to go up, but his wife stopped him. Jim did not want to sit around and wait for the unexpected to take place. He told his wife that Angela was his daughter, and when a man's heart was broken, he was capable of anything. He reminded his wife of the outcome of what happened between Angela and her ex. The man who tried to kill his daughter for leaving him. Jim was not waiting around until Sebastian snapped. Jim made his way up the staircase.

Angela couldn't find the right words to offer Sebastian. She knew nothing that she would have said would have eased Sebastian's pain, so she stood in silence. After not getting any response, Sebastian swung the door open, and to his surprise, Jim was standing in front of him. Sebastian stormed past him, brushing Jim on his shoulder. Angela sat back in the chair and tears dripped into her bosom.

Sebastian swiftly walked down the stairs. The best man was standing at the end of the stairway, along with Angela's mom, waiting for him to hit the bottom of the stairs. Some of the guests had left after Angela's dad said there wasn't going to be a wedding that day. Sebastian's close relatives, friends and a few co-workers stayed around to make sure he was okay, and Satin was one of them.

"Yo, Se… what up, money? Is everything okay, bruh?" the best man, Rome, asked as Sebastian reached the bottom of the stairway.

"Sebastian, honey, is everything okay? You guys are still getting married today, right? Please tell me that you are," Mrs. Winfield asked, still full of concern.

*****

Jim consoled Angela as she wept into her daddy's arms. He was the only one in the room with Angela when she decided she couldn't go through with the wedding. Jim comforted his daughter and told her that if that was what she really felt in her heart, then she shouldn't go through with the nuptials. Jim expressed it was better that she realized that then, instead of later.

Jim knew how Angela really felt, and as a father, he wanted his daughter to do what was best for her and what made her happy. Jim had a sense of empathy for Sebastian, but at the end of the day, no man was good enough for his precious Angie, and it was his daughter that he was concerned about, although she had only given him partial of the truth of the reason for her decision on not wanting to marry Sebastian.

Jim informed his wife of everything Angela shared with him, but she was hoping that Sebastian's time alone with Angela would change Angela's mind. Unfortunately for the young couple, Mrs. Winfield was wrong. Her daughter had other plans for her life and it didn't include Sebastian Smith.

Sebastian was immeasurably hurt; he couldn't even mumble a word. He swiftly swiped both of his hands across the table that was in the middle of the foyer, filled with the wedding programs and a basket of rice, wrapped of net and a bow, that the guests were supposed to throw at the couple once married. The papered programs flew everywhere, and the basket of rice hit the floor, which startled everyone.

Sebastian stormed out of the church. He jumped into the white Rose Royce he rented that would take him and his wife to be to their designated reception hall.

Mrs. Winfield stormed up the staircase to go see about Angela. The best man informed the rest of the wedding party that indeed there was not going to be a wedding that day. The church was left hollowed. A wedding that was supposed to take place that evening, didn't.

Chapter Four

Momma's Baby, Daddy's Maybe

When Satin was thrown out of her parents' home, she tossed her pride aside and lived in the woman's shelter for a year before she could afford her own spot. During that time, she managed to finish high school, attend college and get a job at McCarren Airport, cleaning the bathrooms when she was a couple of weeks pregnant with Noah.

Satin eventually saved all her earnings, and got herself an apartment. By then, three years had passed and things started to slowly turn around for her when she landed a job at Bank of America as a teller; thanks to a lady who worked at the shelter, who she kept in contact with. The lady had convinced her husband to get Satin a job where he worked.

Bishop hadn't seen or spoken to Satin since he had cast her out of the house. Satin worked very hard to right her wrongs, and tried to figure out a way she could get back into her father's good graces. A safe-haven, the one she always had as a child. Sadly, that place of safety was no longer available to her. Bishop was still as stern as they came. Satin wasn't trying to move back into the house that she was thrown out of, but hated that she and her father no longer had a relationship. That broke Satin's heart.

Satin needed the extra financial help, so she moved the father of her child Nolan in, and word quickly got out to Bishop that his daughter had shacked up. Once again, Satin had disobeyed Bishop's order of the Christian family, and he still wanted nothing to do with his daughter, whom was playing house and still living in sin. Bishop wanted nothing to do with his grandson Noah, either. Satin acted as if she didn't know shacking up and still living in sin was not a way to go about getting back into Bishop's good graces. If Satin learned anything at all, she knew in Bishop's eyes, she was still thought of as a promiscuous girl, who was on the fast track to the gates of hell and enjoying the ride.

*****

Satin made it home after attending her coworker, Sebastian's, wedding that never happened. Nolan was home that Saturday evening, something he wouldn't normally do. Nolan was in the streets heavy, and Satin gave him the space to come and go as he pleased. She was just happy to have him there, so he could be a part of Noah's life.

"I surely wish you would have come with me to my co-worker's wedding. Well actually, there wasn't a wedding, it was cancelled. Wow! That was sooo crazy, I tell you, but you still should have come."

"You know I don't do weddings. That ain't my type of thing to do, but aye… I'm 'bout to head on out to chill with my homie Que. Hit me up if you need me," Nolan spoke as he slipped into his Timberlands.

"Nolan, you really need to start thinking about other things rather than just hanging with them good for nothing niggas."

"Aye, I don't tell you who or who not to hang out with and you surely ain't 'bout to start that crazy shit with me, ya feel me? I'm a grown ass man out 'chea, and I chill with who I want to chill with!" Nolan boomed.

Satin rolled her eyes. "I'm just saying-- them dudes always up to something no good. I would hate to see you getting caught up in some foolishness."

You surely don't act as if you grew up in a church like myself.

"Let me worry 'bout that. Your job is to worry 'bout Noah, and that's it. Like I said, I'm a grown ass man and I can look out for myself. Fuck I look like needing a woman looking out for me in these streets. I run that shit, and besides, if anything was to ever go down, my homies got my back."

Satin looked at Nolan and began to regret the fact that she had a baby by a knuckle head who didn't want anything out of life but to hang on corners all day and smoke weed with his homies. To Satin's wonder, Nolan behaved as if he sat through Sunday morning bible school and didn't learn a thing. Nolan transformed from a young kid who attended church and bible study with his mom every Sunday, to a young man who didn't care about anything or anyone, but himself.

Nolan worked as a welder, but after his eight hours was up, the streets was where he could be found. Satin didn't regret the fact that Noah was born. She still allowed herself to believe kids were a gift from God, but when she was honest with herself, Satin regretted that she chose to lay down with a guy she thought she knew. It turned out that she knew nothing at all about Nolan and she had gotten herself knocked up as a result. Everything Bishop said about Nolan was true, and he warned Satin to steer clear of the young boy, who had no interest in church at all and was only there because his mother forced him, but Satin was too blinded by lust at the time and couldn't see through the smoke.

Nolan only agreed to move in so he could move out of his momma's house, who was always riding his back about hanging in the streets, and still tried to force him to attend church. Nolan had stopped going all together, just like Satin had chosen to. He told his mother the pastor of her church hated him because he had gotten his daughter pregnant, and he refused to sit in his church knowing that.

Nolan accused Bishop of being a hypocrite and wanted nothing to do with church folks all together. Nolan's mother told him if he didn't serve God living under her roof, he had to move out of her house. Nolan figured moving in with his baby mother would get him from underneath his mother's religious overbearing ways and would give him a little more freedom to live how he pleased.

Nolan figured that he could also do his part for Noah, financially, because Nolan's free time was always spent with his homies. Nolan and Satin shared the responsibilities of the bills, with Satin pinching in a bit more, and made due with what they had. Nolan was nowhere ready to be anyone's father, but he called himself stepping up to the plate and taking care of his daddy responsibility.

Satin accepted Nolan's behavior because she really needed the financial help. She made enough at the bank to cover her living expenses, but it left her broke after she paid all the bills and left her with nothing extra to play with. She no longer received government assistance with food, because she made over the allowed amount at the bank.

Satin dropped out of college after receiving her Associate's degree to work full time, but had plans on returning to obtain her Bachelor's once Noah got a little older; he was only three at the time.

Satin convinced herself that maybe Nolan would learn to value and appreciate her, and change his street mentality by committing to building a real family with her and their son. Satin greatly feared being another young black single mother raising a fatherless man child. Nolan's priorities were not in order, and he wasn't ready for the things that Satin was ready for. It was the hard knock life hand that she had dealt herself, but Satin was determined to turn things around for the sake of Noah and herself.

Whatever, jackass. Keep thinking them niggas got your back.

"Well, Noah and I will be here when you get back, I guess. I really didn't plan on being back this early, but as I've said, the wedding didn't happen. It is such a beautiful day today; it surely would be nice to take our son to the park or something."

"Park? Yeah, that would be nice. Go on and do that. Take Noah to the park and buy him a ball or something to play with while he's out there," Nolan said as he pulled five dollars out of his wallet, set it on the table, and walked out the door.

Really dude? What was I thinking to EVER get caught up with a joker like that? Something's gotta give, man.

"That's okay, though... Mommy and you will take us a little nap, then to the park we go," Satin said as she picked Noah up and raised him in the air.

Satin tossed him a bit as Noah giggled with saliva falling out of his mouth. Satin took Noah's pajamas off and slipped him on something comfortable to play in at the park.

Satin placed Noah in his crib which was transformed into a toddler bed and undressed herself, too. She then slipped into yoga pants and a fitted tee so she could get a walk in around the park. Satin reached into Noah's bed and picked him up and placed him in the bed with her. Satin was well aware that Noah was no longer an infant, but she treated him as if he was still attached on to her breast for a feeding. Noah was her baby, her one and only, and Satin wasn't ready to accept the fact that he was growing up.

Noah played with his favorite Marvel action figure, and after a while got down from the bed and played with other toys. Satin's cell phone rang, momentarily breaking up their mother and son time.

"Hello," Satin answered.

"Bestie? What the hell happened today? I heard ya boy Sebastian was left standing at the altar all by his lonesome," Brandy asked.

Brandy worked at the bank with Satin and Sebastian, who was a tax accountant. Brandy was also a teller. She and Satin were cool, but far from best friends. Brandy addressed everyone as bestie;

it was just her friendly personality. Satin didn't dislike Brandy, but she didn't fully trust Brandy nor did they hang out outside of work.

Satin didn't quite understand why Brandy called everyone her bestie or why in the hell did she mind everybody's business. Brandy was very talkative, the total opposite of Satin. Satin was sociable only with people she trusted. Something about Brandy didn't sit well with her. All Brandy would do was brag about how many guys she was sleeping with, and how she made them pay her bills.

Satin didn't respect Brandy. Not because she judged Brandy, but because she knew firsthand what it felt like to be judged. Satin didn't respect some of the choices Brandy made, and the fact that she bragged about them just didn't make any sense. Satin had a modest, laid back type of personality in oppose to Brandy's outgoing one.

"News surely does travel fast, doesn't it? Why didn't you just come to the wedding?" Satin questioned.

"I had to work. How will the bank function properly if all the employees were at a wedding that never happened? So, what happened?"

"Well, as you already obviously know, the wedding didn't happen today. It is true that Sebastian was left at the altar. I feel so bad for the poor guy. The look in his eyes when the bride's father showed up at the altar, instead of her, was heart breaking. He seems to be such a sweet person. I don't know what happened between him and the bride to be, but no, they didn't get married today as planned."

"Man, I can't even imagine what homie is going through. I don't know much about him, other than anything work related. I've flirted with him a time or two, but he didn't bite. I guess it was because he had plans on getting married. He's probably drowning himself in a bottle of Hennessy or some shit right about now."

"You think? The man indeed had plans of getting married, duh. I don't know much about him either, other than that he's one of the accountants; he looks much younger than the others he always has lunch with. I know if it were me, I probably would be doing the same thing, and I don't even drink. I'm sure he's devastated; anybody would be."

"Right. He doesn't say much to us, other than good morning ladies. I was rather surprised that he invited everyone to his wedding, to tell you the truth."

"I guess it was the *appropriate* thing to do. I love weddings, so I went."

"I don't; too damn emotional and overrated if you'd ask me. Well, I guess I'll see you on Monday. I'm about to get ready for my date with Trevor."

"Trevor? I thought you said the two of you broken up?"

"We did, but that doesn't mean I can't still have an ongoing relationship with his wallet. He's taking me shopping *before* dinner, and I need him to give me five hundred dollars on my rent."

Satin slightly chuckled. "You know what? I can't with you; I just can't, bye Brandy.

Chapter Five
This Thing We Call Life

Monday quickly came and went, and soon came Friday morning. Satin went to meet Carolyn so she could watch the baby. Noah's day care center was closed and under investigation after one of the workers was caught beating a couple of kids on camera. As soon as Satin got wind of the incident, she snatched Noah right out of day care, and begged her mother to watch him just for one week while she searched for a new day care. Carolyn knew she would be taking a huge risk of causing conflict between her and Bishop, but once again, Carolyn could not just stand by and not help Satin.

Carolyn had been watching her grandbaby for one week at the house behind Bishop's back. After Bishop would leave out for work, she would let Satin drop Noah off. Surprisingly, Bishop came home early Thursday evening with plans of holding a Men's Conference later that evening at the church. Carolyn knew of the

Men's Conference, but it slipped her mind with the busy body of a three-year-old. Bishop mentioned it to her a month prior, but Carolyn soon forgot.

Bishop walked in and caught Carolyn right in the act. His feelings did not budge, and nothing had changed between him and Satin still. Bishop took one long look at Noah, and instantly recognized who he was.

Noah was a spitting image of his daddy, Nolan, but he had his mother's smooth chocolate skin and soft curly hair. It reminded Bishop of when he first laid eyes on Satin when she was born, and it saddened him deeply. Bishop was the one to name his daughter, Satin, because her skin and hair reminded him of a black glistening scarf his wife would always wear when she was pregnant that radiated pure grace and beauty.

Bishop observed Noah for a second, being that it was his very first time laying eyes on his bastard grandson. Bishop didn't speak one word for a long time; he just stared. Carolyn pleaded with Bishop to hold his grandson, but he couldn't move a muscle or utter a word; he just stared in bewilderment. Carolyn thought that by him finally seeing his grandson, Bishop would have a change of heart and the family could mend the broken fences. Bishop had a twinkle in his eyes, the same as he had when he saw Satin for the first time, but it wasn't enough to change his hardened heart.

Carolyn left to meet Satin, as that was their arrangement in the evenings. Bishop waited until Carolyn came back, and told her that she better not *ever* disobey him in that way again. He knew of Carolyn's visits to see Satin and Noah, and that didn't concern him one bit, because Carolyn was Satin's mother, and Bishop knew she could never turn her back on their daughter completely; Carolyn was that kind of woman and that was what he loved most about her.

Bishop also knew that he and his wife showed love differently; where Carolyn was understanding, and nurturing, he was tough and stern. It was just who Bishop was and he wasn't changing. He wasn't even the least bit ashamed of the man he was, a proud man of God.

Carolyn pleaded with her husband to please reconsider, and to somehow find it in his hardened heart to forgive and get over what happened because Noah was born and there was no changing the fact. Bishop expressed that he had forgiven his daughter the night he found out what Satin had done, and he still loved her more than anything, but his house was his house, and what he said went. Satin and the child she had out of wedlock were not welcomed there. Bishop was convinced that the daughter he raised in the church was still behaving promiscuously, and he wanted no part of it. He warned Carolyn. Satin had not learned from her mistakes, because if she had, she wouldn't have continued sinning by having premarital sex, and living with a man whom she was not married to and had no respect for Christian values.

Carolyn reminded Bishop that even Jesus sat and ate with sinners, so why couldn't he just do the same? Bishop responded by saying that he and his house would serve the Lord. And if anyone, including his own child, could not respect that, the sinner was not welcomed into his home bringing unwanted demonic spirits.

Bishop still could not see past his strict religious beliefs; stubborn as a mule, his wife believed. No matter what Carolyn said or done, she still could not change Bishop's mind, and she wasn't pleased with her husband by any means.

*****

When Carolyn called Satin the next morning, she told her what happened between her and Bishop the evening before. Carolyn explained to Satin that she would have called and told her the day before, but she was emotionally drained and couldn't do anything but pray like never before.

Carolyn stated that she was tired of the strife between Satin and her father, and it was time that one of them reached out to the other. Satin expressed to Carolyn how much she loved her father, but she didn't have anything to say to him after what he had done to her and she no longer believed her father loved her.

Carolyn tried to convince Satin that she was just as wrong as Bishop by not forgiving him, and God was not pleased with her as well. Between Bishop and Satin, Carolyn was exhausted; spiritually and emotionally. The brokenness in the family was consuming her greatly.

Satin didn't know what she was going to do about a babysitter for the day. She had nowhere else to go, Nolan was at work already, and she would have died of a slow death first before she took Noah back to his old nursery. Satin searched all week for another day care, but they all were full in her area and wouldn't have an opening for a couple of months.

Satin dressed for work anyway and dressed Noah. She wrecked her brain for a temporary solution, but didn't know what she was going to do. Satin thought about bringing Noah to work with her, but knew she would be breaking the rules.

Overwhelmed, Satin walked out the door, thinking she would figure something out. She couldn't even make it down the stairs good enough with Noah by the hand. She glided on the staircase and dramatically broke down with Noah landing next to her.

"Why must this keep happening to me, Lord?! Why?! The more I try, the more I fall! I can't keep doing this, this is too much! Why does that man hate me so much, I am his daughter!" Satin cried out to God with a face filled with overflowing crocodile tears.

Noah's little hands wiped his mother's tears as he stared at her crushing like a defenseless little child. His three-year-old mind couldn't fully grasp what was going on, all Noah knew was that his mommy was crying. Noah hugged Satin. She sat Noah on her lap and embraced him into her bosom; just as her mother would do to her as a child.

Satin rocked slowly back and forth. "I'm so sorry baby, it's okay. Mommy's okay. I'm so sorry for scaring you, okay man, but mommy is sad right now. I love you. Mommy loves you more than anything or anyone else in this world and I will do better. I promise, Mommy will do better, okay?"

I must get it together for the sake of my son.

Not fully understanding what his mother was saying, other than sensing she was unhappy because of her tears, Noah took his little hand and brushed it up against his mother's cheek, cleaning some of her tears away.

"Okay, Mommy," Noah softly muffled.

Drenched in sadness, his tiny lips brushed Satin on her wet jaw; just as she would do to him when Noah would cry after a bad fall and Satin would give him a magic kiss on his boo-boo and tell him that everything would be okay.

Satin struggled to put on a gentle smile, to assure Noah that she was okay, and to give him some form of relief, if possible. She silently acknowledged the tightness in her chest by placing her hand on her rib cage as she watched her baby boy take in all her despair; it broke Satin's heart immensely. She mumbled underneath her breath as she mutely cried out to God and asked for his forgiveness and help.

Satin and Noah continued to sit on the stairs; desolate and inflicted.

Karen, one of Satin's neighbors, strode up to the stairway that led the way to her apartment door. Karen noticed her neighbor, Satin, the young girl with the adorable little boy, who spoke to her every time she saw her, looking as though something was wrong.

Karen had just gotten back from her morning run to the grocery store. She held a brown paper bag filled with milk, eggs, bread and snacks. Instead of bypassing Satin and going straight to her apartment, Karen stopped without hesitation.

"Good morning, sweetheart. Is everything okay?" Karen spoke in a warm concerned tone.

Satin recognized Karen as the older lady who always wore a warm smile on her face, and would have a snack for Noah when they would see her outside. Karen also would rub Noah's hair and tell Satin how sweet of a boy Noah was, who reminded her of her son when he was his age and her grandson, who was also Noah's age.

With a tired sad tone, Satin answered, "Good morning, Mrs. Karen. Yeah, I'm fine," she lied.

"Well, that doesn't sound like your fine to me," Karen sassed as she switched arms with the paper bag. Karen reached her hand out to Noah, and he placed his hand inside of hers.

"You and your mommy come with me. I don't know what's going on, but Mrs. Karen has something to make Mommy feel better, and something really special for you."

Noah stepped out of Satin's lap and stood to his feet.

"I know what you have for me!" Noah spoke with excitement in a delicate essence.

"You dooo? What does Mrs. Karen have for such a smart little boy such as yourself?"

"A snack!" Noah clapped his hands as his face lit up like the Kool Aid kid.

Noah remembered Mrs. Karen to be the nice lady who always gave him treats.

"You are absolutely right! Come on with me, sweetie," Karen advised Noah and looked at Satin. She nodded her head for her to come along as well.

Satin glanced at her watch, and realized she was almost late for work. Getting to work on time was the least of her worries; she still didn't know what she was going to do with Noah. Satin realized at some point she was going to have to call her boss, who had no sympathy for working mothers at all because she wasn't a parent herself.

Satin softly smirked at Karen. She stood to her feet and rid her backside of the foot printed dust that plagued the cement. Satin followed Karen as her and Noah led the way to her apartment, which was right across the way from her very own door.

Karen walked into the apartment and went straight to the kitchen. Her apartment was as clean as a five-star hotel and had a hospitable appeal; fuzzy and warm, just like most grandmothers' homes did.

The smell of a mouth-watering country breakfast smothered the scent of the kitchen. Karen sat her bag on the table, and started to remove her groceries from the bag. She opened the box with mini packs of golden graham cookies and gave a packet to Noah.

"Thank you," Noah smiled.

"You're welcome, sweetie. You and Mommy can have a seat right here at this table. Wait... did the baby have his breakfast already? I don't want to ruin his appetite by giving him cookies."

"Uh no, actually he hasn't. Noah would normally get his breakfast at day care."

"I'm sorry, Noah. Mrs. Karen didn't know that; me and my big mouth. Ahhh... you know what... how 'bout I fix you a nice bowl of hot sweet cinnamon oatmeal and a cold glass of orange juice, and thennnn you can have your sweet graham cookies afterwards? Would you like that? Is that okay, Mommy?" Karen peered over at Satin.

"Oh no, Mrs. Karen, you don't have to do that; we don't want to cause you any trouble. We really have to get going, but I do need to make an important phone call right quick."

I guess I'll call off, and that way I can fix Noah some breakfast at home. Mrs. Karen is such a sweet person; I hate to be bothersome.

"Aw sweetheart, you and little Noah could never cause me any trouble. I was already going to make breakfast. My grandson is on his way over. I baby sit him for his parents while they work. Trust me, if Mee-Maw don't have his oatmeal when he comes over, I would not hear the end of it. I've already cooked the turkey bacon and eggs before my run to the grocery store, before I realized I was out of milk. Go on, make your call. This little handsome fella and I will make the oatmeal. Oh and… would you like a hot cup of coffee or anything? There's also tea, milk and orange juice?"

"No Ma'am, thank you, I'm fine. Are you sure, Mrs. Karen, because I was just about…"

"Yes, I'm sure. Go on and make your phone call, darling," Karen politely interrupted. "You may step into the living room if you need some privacy. We will still be right here when you return," Karen swayed her hand in the air for Satin to go on and make her call.

Satin smiled at Karen and peered at Noah, as she noticed his face ignited at Mrs. Karen for always being so nice to him. "Okay then, since you insist, Noah can have some oatmeal. I'll step into the living room for a minute. I'm just calling my job, really. Noah, sweetheart—Mommy's just going right in the living room to make a quick phone call, okay baby? I'll be right back."

"You young first time mommies are so cuteee; I tell you the truth. Go on, he's fine. I promise, I won't let him slip out that chair and bust his bottom. I'll make sure to catch him with one hand right before his head grazes that very hard ceramic floor. Little man won't even remember what happened, I promise."

Satin smiled. She knew Karen was toying with her. She stepped out of the room and made the phone call.

"Thanks for calling Bank of America. How may I direct your call?

"Janice, please."

"I'm sorry, Janice is in her morning meeting. Would you like to leave a message?"

"Rayanne?"

"Yes, this is Rayanne. How may I assist you, please?"

"This is Satin, Rayanne. Will you please let Janice know that I won't be in today? I have an emergency with my son and I'll give her a call back after lunch to inform her more about what's going on."

"Hi Satin. Sure, I'll be certain to relay that as soon as Janice is done with the meeting. Is the baby okay?" Rayanne asked, full of sincerity; she had far more empathy than Janice would ever display.

"Yeah, he's fine; thanks for asking. It's just-- something came up at the day care."

"Oh okay, I'll be sure to give Janice your message then. See you on Monday, Satin."

"Thanks, Rayanne, see you Monday."

Satin pressed end call on her phone. She walked back into the kitchen. Karen was standing at the stovetop in an apron, stirring the oatmeal. Noah was watching cartoons on the TV, sipping orange juice.

"Nah, I ain't tryna get all up in your business and what not, and I don't expect you to just tell me what was going on with you when I walked up to the staircase and found you crying, but I will ask you-- are you and this baby okay, and is there anything, or any way I can help?"

Karen never turned around; she stood facing the stove. Noah's attention was glued to the television. He was lost in the show 'Caillou'. Satin thought briefly about not sharing her personal problems with someone she barely knew, other than speaking to Karen when she would pass by. Satin didn't want to trouble anyone with her problems other than her mother, but Karen reminded her of all the good things about Carolyn in a sense. Karen was very motherly with any and everyone who came into her presence. The warm loving woman couldn't help herself.

After chasing her thoughts around in circles in her head, Satin finally answered.

"Uhhh no, I'm not okay," she let out a deep sigh. "Um… I just had to call off work, because I don't have a babysitter for Noah. There was an accident at his nursery last week and I pulled him out. Now, I'm having trouble finding another one."

"Well, say no more. Look at him, I think sweet little Noah wants to stay right here with Mrs. Karen, doesn't he?" She looked over at Noah.

"Yay! Can I stay Mommy, please, can I stay?" Noah wiggled in the chair with excitement.

"Mrs. Karen, I can't just impose on you like that. You are doing way too much as it is. No, I couldn't do that. Besides, I've already called off."

Karen placed the top on the steaming oatmeal. She removed the towel from across her shoulder, and cleaned her hands. Karen then placed the towel on top of the pot of oatmeal as it sat, cooling off. She slowly turned around.

"Let me ask you something, baby."

"Sure," Satin answered as she stood and folded her hands across her chest.

"Do you believe in God?"

"Uh yeah, of course I do."

How can I not, I was raised by a pastor, but I won't even go into all of that. I'm emotionally exhausted.

"Do you believe He knew what you needed before you knew it? Do you believe that it wasn't a coincidence that I found you sobbing your little heart out on the stairway? Do you also know that God uses people to bless others?"

"Uhhh yes… I do, but it's just…"

"No buts, is it or is it not true? You're gonna go on and carry your little precious self on to work, you hear? Noah will be fine right here with me and my grandson. I've already told you, I babysit my grandson during the week for his parents, which I really don't consider keeping my own grandchild babysitting. It's more like-- us just spending quality time together, and besides, he's Mee-Maw's company since I lost my husband. But don't you feel sorry for me, because I talk to God all day, every day and I understand that he's always with me."

Tears started to saturate Satin's eyes. "Why are you so nice to us? I don't understand. No one has never ever been this nice to me, other than my mother."

Chapter Six

Joy Comes in the Morning

Karen's heart was filled with compassion for the young girl who lived across the hall from her. She remembered what it was like for her as a young mother, and Karen could do nothing but sympathize with Satin. It didn't hurt that Karen was also a Christian woman.

Karen walked over to Satin and cuddled her. "It's okay, baby. We all have been where you are at some point in our lives. I understand what it's like trying to work and raise a child. It's not an easy thing to do, and we all can use a helping hand at times. It's okay, you will be okay. Your heavenly father has got you covered, and this I know because the bible tells *all* of us so."

"But I don't even know your full name or your background history with handling children," Satin cried.

"You know the most important things. I live right across the hall from you. I was living here when you moved here a year ago, I really don't believe you think I'll run off with Noah, do you?"

"No, I don't, but it's just..."

"There you go with them buts again, young lady. My full name is Karen Ann Murphy. When you get a minute… what is that thing all you young people use today? Goggle, Ogle."

"Google?"

"Yeah, that old darn thing. Use that phone you have, and Google me. My husband died five years ago, I live alone as you know, because as you and I both know, I'm your neighbor. You see me and who comes to my home. My sister visits time to time, and my two children. My son, who should have been here by now, but I guess will be here in a minute, and my daughter, when she's not busy with that fancy job of hers."

A sound of the living room door opening made its way through the apartment. Karen's son, Darrius, walked into the kitchen, holding a little boy in his arms.

"Hi Mother," Darrius spoke in a deep tone as he leaned in and placed a peck on his mother's cheek. "Hello," Darius continued as he noticed Satin.

She returned the hello.

"Hey, baby. You running late this morning, I see. I was expecting you guys thirty minutes ago."

"Traffic was a bit jammed this morning, ma'am. I really must run before I'm late for work, though. I wish I had time to have whatever that is your cooking. Probably oatmeal, but it smells so good in here! I smelled it before I even came in from outside the front door."

"Yep, you know it. Mee-Maw must have her baby some oatmeal. Good morning, sugah." Karen reached in and pecked her grandson on the forehead. Darrius Jr. reached out his hands for his grandmother to hold him, but Karen just played with his hand instead as Big Darrius continued to hold him. Karen took her attention back to Darrius.

"You're the boss, you'll be fine." Karen dismissed his statement about running late. "Son, this is my friend Satin, and that's her son Noah over there. Today is Noah's first day here with me. He will be joining Lil Darrius and I."

"It's nice to meet you, Satin. What's up, lil man?" Darrius walked over and rubbed the top of Noah's head. "Satin, I'm telling you now, and I'm only telling you this because my wife and I go through this everyday with our son. My mother is going to spoil your boy rotten. He won't even want to come home with you when you come back to pick him up. I'm just sayin'," Darrius joked.

Satin chuckled. "I can see that already. Mrs. Karen has already spoiled his butt even before today. Every time we leave out of the door, Noah's looking for Mrs. Karen because she always has a snack for him."

"See… well, you already know what it is then. I ain't even got to get into it," Darrius chuckled. "But rest assure, your boy is in very, very good hands. My mother is really good with my son and the other kids she has babysat over the years as well."

"I can believe that. Wait, so… you babysat other kids, too, Mrs. Karen?"

"Not anymore, really. Just my grandson, and on occasions when one of the parents of the kids whom I use to babysat needs me. You know… like in situations like yours; pulling out of day care and waiting until another becomes available."

"I see." A gentle smiled appeared on Satin's face.

"Well, it was nice meeting you, Satin. See you later, tough guy." Darrius hugged and kissed little Darrius, then sat him in the chair next to Noah. "Alright lil man, see you later, too." He meshed Noah's hair again.

Noah smiled.

"I'm gone, Ma." Darius walked out of the kitchen.

"See you later Son, love you!"

"Love you too, Mother!" Darrius screamed from the living room, and out the door he went.

"So… do we have a deal? I'll watch Noah today, and as for long as you may need a babysitter, or until you find another day care."

"Yes, we have a deal, Mrs. Karen. How much? I don't get paid until next Friday. I can pay you then."

"Don't you worry your little pretty self with that. You've had enough to worry about for one day as is; tomorrow will take care of itself. We can always revisit that one, okay?"

"Okay, Mrs. Karen," Satin hugged her. "You are truly a blessing in disguise, thank you so much. You have no idea how much I appreciate you."

"Oh, dear, I think I do. I'm sure if it was the other way around, you would do the same for me. You seem like a really nice girl and all."

"Yes ma'am, I would in a heartbeat."

"Nah go on now. Get on out of here. Me and these two little fellas about to eat us some oatmeal, and have bible study after breakfast. We may even watch cartoons and only God knows what else they'll have me in here doing, but I'm ready!" Karen stated with much enthusiasm and positive attitude.

Satin noticed a children's bible on the kitchen counter.

Well that explains the reason for the bible. Truly a great spirit, thank you Lord.

"Okay, okay, I'm going; say no more."

Satin walked over to Noah and gave him a tight clasp and a kiss. She told Noah she'd be back later as soon as she finished work. Satin toyed with Karen's grandson for a second, and felt at ease about her decision to leave Noah.

Satin gave Karen Noah's bag with a change of clothing and Noah's favorite superhero action figures to play with. She also gave Karen the number to her cell and work in case she needed to call. Satin hugged Karen once more. Karen fixed her a to go breakfast and out the door Satin went.

Satin was relieved she could go to work. She was treading on thin ice with her boss, Janice, because she'd taken off a couple of times before when Noah was sick. No matter how much Satin explained to Janice about Noah's situation, Janice was still the witch riding her broomstick and didn't have patience for excuses, nor did she thrive off self-pity and sad stories.

Before the bank position, Janice had only been out of the military for a year, and had been supervising army cadets most of her time spent in the military. Janice handled everything, and everyone, as if they were on the front line about to go to war. 'The General' was how they all referred to Janice around the bank when she wasn't looking. They all knew better to do it in front of her face or The General would end up on a warpath.

Satin was in for a rude awakening!

Chapter Seven
Meet the General

At the bank, there were still plenty of whispers between the
employees of what happened at the wedding of their co-worker,
Sebastian. Satin didn't really entertain the petty gossip; it just didn't
faze her one way or another. She had only spoken to Brandy about it,
and that was merely because Brandy called inquiring. Brandy, on the
other hand, was always in the midst of the gossip and that was why
Satin only trusted her as far as she could see her.

Sebastian had not returned to work since the wedding that
never happened. Neither was he away in Hawaii on the honeymoon
that was planned for him and Angela. Their honeymoon was not
scheduled until the following week, because that was the only time
Angela could take her vacation from work. To put it off by a week
was their mutual agreement. Sebastian was looking forward to

relaxing on the beautiful island with leis and alcoholic umbrella drinks.

Satin strolled in an hour late. She didn't call to warn Janice that she had decided to show up after getting a babysitter. Satin stood at her teller line, which was also known as the teller's private cage. Janice was in the back office and had not noticed Satin's arrival. She got word from Rayanne that Satin showed up unexpectedly.

To Janice's dismay, Satin had called off and she had filled her cage with another employee who was in training to become a teller. When Satin arrived, she advised the trainee that she would take over, but she could stick around to continue to learn as much as possible about how the front office of the bank was ran.

Janice immediately trailed from the back once she heard Satin was in her cage. "Follow me to my office, now!" Janice roared. She then took her attention off Satin and focused on the new girl. "Cindy, you can continue to cover this lane. If you are unsure about any transaction, before you proceed, see Brandy and she'll assist you, and I do mean BEFORE you proceed. Do I make myself clear?" Janice bellowed.

"Yes, I understand completely," Cindy answered as Janice's intimidation had taken its course with her as well.

Satin just kept quiet and followed Janice as she insisted. She didn't like the way Janice had raised her voice at her, but didn't feel that she had grounds to dispute the disrespect being that she had come in late after calling off. Satin and Janice marched to the back office, and Janice closed the door behind them. Janice took a seat behind her stiff desk as Satin continued to stand.

"I don't know what kind of games you think you're playing, but your services are not needed here today. It has been filled after your call in. It isn't fair to the teller who has already fulfilled such duty. As a matter of fact, I'm placing you on a suspension without pay for one week, and upon your return, you will be placed on an in-house temporary suspension for one month to determine if your job here at Bank of America is still active. Your performance includes no taking off under no circumstances, on time daily, and exceptional performance with the customers. You will receive no warnings after this, no written statement, just a pink slip if I feel you failed your assessment. You have been informed. Is there anything I've said that you do not understand?" Janice spoke with a serious gawk.

"Um… let me just say, I'm not playing any kind of games. I came to work because…."

Janice interrupted Satin. "I'm really not interested in why you decided to come in, Satin. The question was… is there anything I've said that you do not understand?"

"Well, excuse me. I guess I misunderstood your question," Satin spoke with sarcasm. "Um… what about hospitalization? If my son or I is hospitalized, how can I possible come in for work under the circumstances?"

"I guess you'll just have to hope that doesn't happen. No excuses will be accepted; that's final," Janice spoke.

You Witch. I never disliked a person as much as I dislike your ass.

"I guess there's nothing else to discuss about this. I understand," Satin spoke as she tried to remain calm and not let Janice's callous attitude provoke her in any way.

"Farewell then. You are dismissed for the rest of the day, and I do mean you can leave the premises," Janice ordered as she turned her back and reached in the file cabinet for Satin's folder. Janice began to document her decision for suspending Satin and add it to the case she had been building against Satin since her first tardiness.

Satin rolled her eyes and walked out of Janice's office. She grabbed her purse and proceeded to leave. At the time, there wasn't a customer in sight; the bank was empty.

"Hey, you're leaving? You just got here," Brandy inquired.

"Um, yeah, I'm leaving. I'll talk to you later," Satin answered, not wanting to get into what just happened.

"Okay, doll. Call me."

Satin smiled at Brandy and walked out of the bank. She walked to her car and sat in the seat. Satin turned the engine key and couldn't even pull out the bank's parking lot. She began to worry about her getting fired and what it was going to be like with no pay for a week. Although Nolan pitched in on the responsibilities, she still had bills to pay.

"JESUS! This just doesn't get any better, do it? Damn! Way to go Satin, way to go."

Satin had a lot on her mind and didn't know what she was going to do about her job or how she could change the unwelcoming relationship between her and the woman who had the power to cost her her livelihood.

Satin drove around for a while and she even thought about looking for a new job. She knew for certain that Noah came first no matter what, and she could always get another job if it came down to that. Satin really liked her job at the bank, other than the fact that her boss was gunning for her head.

Although Satin felt as though her world was tumbling down again, she thought about everything Karen had said to her earlier that morning, and instantly, she started to feel as though her problems would somehow work themselves out. With questions swooping around in her head, Satin's thoughts wandered to Sebastian and what he must have been going through while dealing with a broken heart. She also realized she had not seen Sebastian through the glass window of his office. Satin knew she had problems of her own, but realized there was always someone elsewhere who was going through something worse, and Sebastian was one of them.

Satin ceased her cell phone and called Brandy. "Hey girl. I need a huge favor?"

"What's up chick? What can I do for you, but before that… what happened in The General's office and why did you come in, only to leave?"

"Nothing much really, besides the fact that she suspended me."

"Shut up! No, that bitch did not suspend you, right? When the bank is crowded, your line is the one that moves the fastest. Her ass will regret that once noon gets here and we get that lunch time rush. Today is Friday, too; don't even get me started on the after-work check cashers. You and I both know the new trainee won't be able to handle that."

"Tell me about it, but that is no longer my worry or concern at the moment. I have other things I need to think about like finding a new job."

"Noooo… you can't leave me here with that crazy person by myself. Who will I chill with to pass time, and not be reminded about why I hate working at this location? I should have stayed where I was."

"Yeah, you should have. You may even need to start thinking about putting in a transfer *back* to the other location. I know I would if I were you."

"You know it ain't that easy; better said than done. So, any who… what you needed my help with? I'm taking my fifteen-minute break right now, sooo make it quick."

"Yeah, about that. Well, I noticed the guy Sebastian hasn't returned to work since you know…"

"The wedding that never happened," Brandy clowned around.

"Yeah, that. Anyhow, I kind of feel bad for the guy. I mean, you should have seen him and the look on his face after realizing the woman, whoever she was, wasn't going to marry him. I don't know… I'm just hoping that the guy is okay. I'm certain if the wedding happened he and his wife would probably be on their honeymoon or something by now, but it didn't happen. So, why hasn't he returned to work yet?"

"Hell, if I know, and you keep stressing that as if you really care. What are you getting at, chick?"

Am I?

"I don't know either, but I guess I just want to make sure that he's alright, you know? Like, maybe you can get his number or something."

"I didn't know the two of you were cool like that? Hell, I thought I knew everything that goes on around here, but I guess I don't."

Brandy tooted her lips.

"We're not, silly. I'm just a concerned co-worker, and I just want to give a courtesy call to see if he's okay. There's no harm in that; we are all co-workers, right?"

Although he barely says much to me besides 'good morning' and let's not forget the fact that he always has lunch with the investment bankers, auditors and anyone else around there in a suit.

"I see. A concerned co-worker of a fine ass, young accountant who just so happened to not get married," Brandy teased.

"Girl please, I have a man, you forgot?"

"No, I didn't forget. I'm just saying." Brandy flipped her long blonde straight tresses on both sides of her head.

"Can you get the man's number or not? I just want to call and check up on him. I don't know if anyone else has called from the bank or not. I don't know... I just have this strong feeling that I should."

"Give me a few minutes. When I return to my cage, I'll ask Rayanne for it. She and I are pretty cool, I don't see why she wouldn't consider looking into personnel and giving it to me."

"Okay, great. Call me back when you get it."

"Will do, later babes."

Satin and Brandy ended their call. She pulled over and parked as she waited for Brandy to call her back. Satin noticed the breakfast bag that Karen gave her and got it from the passenger seat.

Earlier, she was so in a hurry to get inside the bank that she forgot about the breakfast. Satin removed the top from the container and started to eat her food.

Dang... this oatmeal is good. This is not no packed oatmeal, I bet Mrs. Karen made this from scratch.

Satin's mind drifted to Karen and she thanked God again for putting her in her life.

The cell phone sounded with a beep and interrupted her thoughts. She tapped the message icon and retrieved the message.

"That was quick."

Satin sat her bowl back into the other seat.

BRANDY: *Sebastian's # 702-555-9845 Be sure to let me know wassup. You got me all worried 'bout ole boy now. LOL Oh and...*

Address: 1440 CANYON LEDGE Court

Vegas of course 89117

SATIN: *Thanks B. I will def do that. I didn't need the address tho.*

BRANDY: *Well, just in case. You never know ;)*

SATIN: *Stop it you! TTYL*

BRANDY: *Later babes!*

"Why would I need this man's address. Brandy's tail is crazy. It's bad enough, I got his phone number without his permission. She does the most."

Satin fetched her food again and finished eating her breakfast. She considered what she would say to Sebastian for placing the call to him without his consent of having his number in the first place. She pondered with ways the conversation could go, but had convinced herself that it didn't matter which way it went, she needed to make sure her co-worker was okay.

Satin called the number Brandy gave to her, but there was no answer. She dialed the number again and still there was no answer. All kinds of thoughts started to enflame her head.

"Hmm… that is weird. I hope Brandy somehow accidently mixed up the orders of the numbers. I would hate to think the poor guy is not okay."

Satin rearranged the numbers a few times and dialed everyone but Sebastian. They just politely told her she had the wrong number. She wanted to call or text Brandy back to ask her whether she had somehow mixed the numbers up, but Satin knew it was Friday, and it was as Brandy said it would be, chaos with the mid-day lunch hour rush.

"This just doesn't make any sense."

Well, you do have his address. The thought popped into her head. "No, I couldn't do that, could I?"

Satin wrestled with her thoughts and the possible boundary she would cross if she did just show up at a person's house without their permission.

MyKisha Mac

Chapter Eight

The Element of Surprise

After teasing with her thoughts for what seemed like forever, Satin finally convinced herself to GPS Sebastian's address. She sat and reflected for a moment before clicking on Start on the navigation and proceeding without caution.

In the back of her thoughts, Satin knew she would be overstepping her boundaries as a co-worker so she attempted to try and talk herself out of it, but the strong sense of urgency she sensed wouldn't go away, instead, it only intensified. Satin didn't understand where the feeling was coming from, but she knew she just had to find out what was going on and that was the only self-briefing she needed.

After driving around for a minute, Satin pulled up in front of Sebastian's brick loft and parked in the driveway. Although it was early afternoon, Sebastian's outside light was on, and a bright light beamed through the plexiglass of the car garage.

This is a really nice area. I'm sure the inside is just as nice as the outside. Only an accountant could afford such a spot.

Satin's eyes slowly scanned around and noticed the flight of stairs that circled the building. "Damn... how far do I have to go up?" *Oh, there's the front door on the second storage.*

Satin's ballerina black flats hit the pavement and she stepped out of the car. She placed her cell phone in the back of her black slacks pocket and sauntered to Sebastian's front door. Satin noticed the door bell and meshed it. She then looked left to right to see if she saw anyone; a neighbor perhaps. When no one answered to the sound of the bell, Satin decided to mesh it again. She waited a few more minutes, then stepped back and gazed up the stairs where there was a veranda. There was no sign of Sebastian, or anyone else for that matter; only empty patio furniture.

Damn... the lights are on, I figured he'd be here. "I guess he's not home."

Satin decided to knock on the door anyway, and to her surprise, the door eased opened after the knock. Her innocent round eyes became wider and she slowly placed her hand on the handle and slightly pushed the door further open.

"Sebastian?" Satin called out in her calm tone, but there was no answer.

What the hell? Why was the door opened? Maybe I should just leave well enough alone.

After thinking for a second, Satin decided to stick her head in and looked around. There still was no sign of Sebastian.

"Hello! Sebastian, are you here?!" Satin called out again.

After standing with her head stuck into the living room of Sebastian's loft, yelling for him and not getting an answer, Satin decided to pull her head back out. She reached in her pocket, got the phone and dialed Brandy. There was no answer. Satin decided to send a Brandy a text.

SATIN: B... I'm here at Sebastian's loft and the door is opened, but I don't see no sign of him. Do you think I should go in?

SATIN: B?

Brandy was busy with customers and couldn't answer her phone, which was right on the shelf at her station. She didn't even notice the flashing light, indicating that she had a new text message. For Brandy, it was work at that time of day as usual.

"Shoot, what am I to do now? This can't be good," Satin uttered as she turned her back to the door and began to walk off.

You can't just leave, go in and see if someone's in there, a foreign thought whispered in her head.

"Like hell, I will," Satin answered her idiotic thought out loud.

Satin played the cat and mouse game with her contemplations for a split second, but then she began to experience the exact urgent feeling she felt before and couldn't totally pull herself away from Sebastian's front door. Lost in unexplainable feelings, Satin's phone then vibrated.

BRANDY: GO IN! YOU'RE THERE ALREADY!

SATIN: OKAY, I'm going. Call me in like 2 minutes tho. I don't know what the hell I may be walking in on.

BRANDY: KK if I can. At work remember?

Satin took a deep breath and exhaled slowly. She decided to step completely inside of Sebastian's loft, but left the door open in case she had to run out because of her unexpected entrance. Whoever was in there, if anybody, if they weren't Sebastian, would have had to catch her because Satin had every intention of hauling ass.

She peeked around and admired the elegant view of the place. She glanced up the stairs to see if she'd see anyone, but it was quiet as a mouse and appeared as though no one was there.

"Sebastian, are you here? This is Satin from Bank of America, I'm coming up! If you don't want me to come up, speak now or forever hold your peace!" she mildly teased.

Shoot… maybe I shouldn't have quoted ANYTHING remotely close to the vowels of marriage. Stupid, stupid, stupid… Satin thought to herself with tightly squeezed eyes.

She then opened her eyes. Satin glanced around the living room again and noticed an entrance into the kitchen. She slowly walked to the kitchen and peeked in before she entered.

"Damn… this sucker is nice. Stainless steel appliances and all. Aww… marbled countertops to match; must be nice."

He must not have any kids, because I don't see not one fingerprint on the refrigerator. Everything in here is as if it's never been touched.

After observing Sebastian's immaculate loft, Satin walked over to the staircase and placed one foot on the bottom stair and slowly proceeded to the next. Satin slowly paced up the stairs and finally reached the top. Her eyes fell on the leather sofa and the three mounted flat screen televisions that were on the wall. There was the largest in the middle and two smaller ones on each side. Satin then noticed the first door.

She walked over and knocked on the door, but got no response. She slowly turned the nob. "An exercising room. Hmm… his own personal gym. Damn…"

There was no sign of Sebastian. Satin closed the door to Sebastian's exercising room. She glanced down the hall and noticed another room door. Satin slowly trailed the hallway and carefully opened the second door.

"Oh wow… a theater room? Nice, but why do you have TVs in the hall if there's a theater room? Only a man." Satin shook her head.

There still was no sign of Sebastian. Satin noticed another door further down the hallway. She tapped on the door and there was no answer. She reached for the knob and hesitated for a second. Her eyes closed and chin fell into her chest.

What are you doing, Satin? Obviously, Sebastian's not here. You should just leave, her conscious told her, but Satin did not listen.

She raised her head and slowly opened the door and her eyes almost popped out of the sockets.

"OH, MY GOD!"

Chapter Nine

Bad Things Follow Good People

Satin slowly walked into the dark room. Her heart was

beating ninety miles a minute and wanted to leap out of her chest. She noticed the body of a naked man, lying flat on his stomach with his head turned facing the entrance of the door. Satin didn't know if Sebastian was dead or alive, but noticed and admired his muscled back and firm ass.

Satin walked closer to the bed.

"Sebastian? Sebastian? Can you hear me?" she called out as she noticed multiple empty bottles of Remy Martin surrounding the bed.

Satin didn't know what to do, she was skeptical. She wanted to leave, but felt she should stay just in case Sebastian was dead and needed the police, or was unconscious and needed some help.

Satin continued to look around the room to see if she saw any signs of foul play that may have happened, but there wasn't any other than empty Champagne Cognac bottles. She looked to see if there was any spilled blood around the room, but there wasn't.

Satin reached over to try and examine the body, purely just by looking, but she couldn't tell much, other than that Sebastian was naked and he obviously trained hard in the gym from the way his muscles ripped through his skin.

Satin rubbed her hands together, trying to spark some warmth because she figured if Sebastian was alive, she didn't want to abruptly wake him from the coldness of her hands. She was sure that he'd jump up swinging, possibly hitting her in the face because she was that close in contact.

After sparking the warmth, Satin then placed her palm on Sebastian's back. The slight up and down rising of his back that she couldn't see with her eyes let Satin knew that he was indeed still alive, but was in a deep sleep. Satin noticed a wine glass tilted on the floor. She carefully bent down and picked it up. She then walked into the master bathroom and stood in front of the sink. Satin saw a reflection of herself in the mirror.

How will you explain this if he jumps up swinging?

Satin turned the faucet on and rinsed out the glass. She then filled the glass with cold water, and walked back to the master bedroom. Sebastian was still lying on the bed and unaware of Satin's visit. Satin tilted the glass over and begun to let the cold water hit Sebastian's face, and then she hurriedly backed out of his reach before his fist met her face.

"The fuck?" Sebastian answered in a low tone, but didn't budge his body. He slightly opened his eyes and glanced at Satin.

"Sebastian, are you okay?"

"Baby… you're here? You came…" he slumbered over his words and squinted his eyes that were playing tricks on him, because all he saw was Angela's face.

"Sebastian, are you okay? Your door was open. I hope you don't mind that I let myself in."

Sebastian didn't respond. He was slowly slipping back into his sleep, and Satin was worried that she wouldn't be able to keep him awake and aware.

"Sebastian?" Satin called out and he didn't answer. She moved back towards the bed and sat next to him. She placed the hunter gray sheet over Sebastian's naked ass; attempting to control the luring thoughts that any woman in her right mind would have had.

Satin tapped Sebastian's back as she called his name again. "Sebastian?"

"Angie…" he mumbled again.

"Angie?"

Oh… that must be her. "No, Sebastian, this is not Angie. I'm Satin, your co-worker from the bank. Are you okay Sebastian? If you are, I'm leaving. I just want to make sure that you are okay before I do," Satin spoke in a sincere tone.

"No…no, don't leave me, baby. Don't leave me again…" Sebastian slurred underneath his breath as he slowly rolled over.

Satin's eyes damn near popped out of her head again. "Oh, my God! Oh, my God!" she coyly covered her eyes.

Damn, this dude's dick is huge. Well at least I know that wasn't the problem in your relationship. Damn… focus Satin, focus.

Sebastian reached his hands out, and placed them on Satin's arms. She sat calmly as her eyes shadowed his hands. Sebastian then swiftly pulled Satin and before she knew it, she was on top of him.

"Uhhh… No no… Sebastian. I am not Angie. I am your cooo-worker. You know, we work together at Bank of America? Bank… me… you… co-worker, do you know who I am?"

"I missed you, baby…" Sebastian muffled as he tried to run his finger through Satin's dark curly hair.

"Oh God, you're delusional. No no… Sebastian. Wake up, Sebastian. I'm leaving, okay? You're fine, so now I can leave," Satin spoke as she tried to wiggle her way from Sebastian's strong hold.

"But why… I gave you everything…"

Okay, this is getting nowhere. "Sebastian, look at me! Open your eyes and look at me!" Satin demanded as she placed both of her fingers on Sebastian's eyelids and pried his eyes opened. "Can you see me now? I'm not Angie, I'm Satin, see?"

Sebastian looked at Satin. He looked at her for a few seconds and didn't speak a word. He was trying to gather his thoughts as he struggled through his drunkenness.

Sebastian had been drinking every day since the wedding day. His best man Rome from Cali had brought some Xanax to try and relax him. Sebastian wasn't a pill popper, but he would have tried anything at the time to numb his pain. Rome was the first to find Sebastian in his state of being, and tried to help him.

Rome came down for the wedding to stand for his friend since childhood as his best man. But the wedding didn't happen and Rome returned to Cali. After calling Sebastian and not receiving an answer, Rome decided to pay him a visit again. He was the one to accidently leave the door unlocked after receiving an emergency call from his baby's mother that his daughter had fallen and broke her collar bone. Rome hurried out of the condo and didn't realize he'd left the door unlocked.

"Heyyy, I know you. What are you doing here?" Sebastian finally spoke after realizing Satin was the cute quiet girl from the bank.

Satin raised herself from off Sebastian and sat back next to him on the bed. Sebastian's eyes kept opening and closing; he was in and out. Satin didn't know that he was also high off Xanax, she believed that he was just drunk.

"Listen… I was there at the church and I… um… just wanted to be sure that you were okay after not seeing you back at work in almost two weeks. I wasn't sure what happened, but now that I know you're okay, I'll go ahead and leave, okay?"

"No, no, don't leave. I ah… Iii…" Sebastian attempted as his stomach rumbled and vomit started to come up in his throat. Satin noticed and quickly raised Sebastian as he then vomited all over her white shirt. She didn't want to risk him choking from his own vomit.

"Oh, my God. This is not happening, ew. This is not happening today." Satin wore a disgusted look upon her face.

"Aw man… I'm sorry…" Sebastian mumbled in his drunkenness as he realized what he had done. He then seemed as though he was going to vomit again.

"Okay, okay… you need to get up."

Satin stood up and grabbed Sebastian by both of his arms and tried to pull him up, but he was way too heavy. His muscled frame was way too much for Satin's petite build.

Sebastian stood to his feet, but wasn't sober enough to stand completely on his own. Satin eased her tiny frame underneath his armpit as Sebastian slung his arm around her shoulder. She slowly struggled to escort Sebastian to the bathroom. He vomited again, but thankfully, it was in the toilet. Satin reached on the chrome towel rack and quickly fetched a face towel. She handed it to Sebastian to wipe his mouth, but he dropped the towel in the toilet.

"Oh, my God, this is not getting any better."

What the heck have I gotten myself into?

"Ughhh..." Sebastian mumbled as he staggered.

"It's okay, I got it, I got you," Satin promised as she reached in the toilet and grabbed the towel by its tip and tossed it into the trash can on the side of the sink.

Sebastian was still struggling to stand. She grabbed his arms again and placed her body underneath his armpit once more. Sebastian's massive tall muscled frame damn near swallowed hers.

Satin removed her phone from her back pocket and placed it on the sink. She then walked Sebastian into the walk-in shower and got in with him. She adjusted the water temperature to warm with one hand as she held on to Sebastian with the other. The splashing water started to hit both of their heads as it washed away the burdens of that day.

Satin's soft curly strands had relaxed a bit when they became wet, and rested on the middle of her back. She had the kind of hair that black people called 'good hair'. It was naturally curly, and when water hit it, it looked like a body wave. If Satin's complexion wasn't gorgeously chocolate, her hair would have misled people to believe she was mixed with another race.

Sebastian was still butt naked and Satin was still fully dressed with vomit stains on her shirt. The warm water rinsed Sebastian's vomit off her chest, but exposed the Cosabella laced bra that she gotten on a sale rack at Kohl's through the shirt.

Satin tried her best to focus on trying to get Sebastian fully aware before she left him in his condition, but she couldn't help the visual of his manhood as the warm water caused it to awaken.

Damn… how do I always manage to get myself into crazy situations?

Chapter Ten

Every Rose Has Thorns

Satin managed to get Sebastian all showered up and helped him brush his teeth; although it was quite the challenge to facilitate a drunken man keeping his balance on a wet surface. She felt accomplished and then covered his goodies with a pair basketball shorts to eliminate the obvious stiff distraction, which was still noticeable through the shorts. Working an eight-hour shift at the bank, standing on her feet all day couldn't compare to managing a strong drunken man.

Satin left Sebastian shirtless and helped him back to bed. She picked up the empty bottles from around the floor and cleaned the vomit that had missed her shirt and had fallen onto the bed. Satin gave Sebastian a bottle of water and made sure he gulped it all. She figured he had to be dehydrated because there was not one bottle of water amongst of the empty liquored bottles. Satin asked Sebastian when was the last time he ate and he told her that he did not remember.

Satin remembered she had left the front door open. She walked to the bathroom, grabbed her phone and placed it back into her pocket. She then walked down to the living room, closed the door and locked it. She then sauntered into the kitchen to see if there was anything in the fridge that she could give to Sebastian to eat before she left. Perhaps a frozen dinner or left overs. Sebastian's refrigerator was filled with water, Gatorade, milk, orange juice and wine, but no sign of any kinds of food of no sort.

"He must eat out all the time? Go figure?"

Satin's phone rang. She closed the refrigerator and answered. "Hello?"

"It's about time you answer the phone, I was beginning to worry. Girl I almost sent them people over there for you."

"What people, Brandy?"

"You know… them people; the police."

Satin slightly laughed. "You're so silly. Well, I'm glad you decided not to, I'm fine."

"Are you sure? I been calling and texting you, but I didn't get an answer."

"Um… yeah, I was uh…" Satin hesitated to tell Brandy what was going on because she knew she would blow everything out of proportion if she found out that her and Sebastian showered together.

"You were uh what?"

"Nothing, Brandy, nothing. I'm uh… I'm getting ready to leave here now."

"So, what happened? Did you find the MIA accountant there inside his home?"

"Yeah, he was here. He was uh… sleeping and um… that's why he didn't hear me calling his name from the door."

"Sleeping, huh? Why do I get this feeling that there's something you are not sharing? Who sleeps that hard and doesn't hear someone calling them or just leaves their front door unlocked?"

"Brandy, the man was in a deep sleep because he's intoxicated. I think he's been drinking every day since the wedding. I found multiply empty bottles of alcohol around the bed. Bye girl, I'm leaving out the door now," Satin lied to rush Brandy off the phone before she became any more suspicious than she already was.

"This conversation is far from over. Call me when you get home."

"It is over, I told you what happened, now bye."

"Later, babes."

Satin and Brandy ended their call. Satin looked through her contacts and dialed Domino's Pizza. She ordered Sebastian some wings and a stuffed chicken parmesan sandwich. She then grabbed a bottle of cold water and walked back to the bedroom.

Sebastian was sitting on the side of the bed with his head down. He appeared to be a bit more aware than what he was before the warm shower.

"Hey, are you okay? I was just about to leave and um…"

Sebastian interrupted, "Yeah, I'm good. Man, I'm sorry that I vomited all over you like that. But, before you go, can I ask you a question?" he spoke, still under the influence, but better off than when Satin found him. The last drink Sebastian had must have come up with his puke.

"Uhhh yeah, sure."

I'm sure you have many, I know I would.

"What are you doing here, and how did you even know where I live?" Sebastian raised his head out of his chest with curious looking eyes.

"That's a good question and I totally understand why you're asking. I um… I noticed you hadn't returned to work after the um… you know, so I don't know, I just got a strange feeling that something may have been wrong."

"Soooo… you just decided to come over?"

"Something like that, but not exactly. I tried calling first, but I didn't get an answer. I don't know… call me crazy I guess, but I needed to make sure you were okay. I um… I was there at the wedding. I'm sorry that things didn't go the way you had planned."

Sebastian put his head down again for a minute. His thoughts flashed back to the day he was left standing at the altar. A tear formed in one of his eyes and slowly fell down his face. He hurried and wiped it before Satin would notice, but she did notice. Her heart went out to Sebastian; she could see the hurt steering from behind his eyes.

Sebastian decided to speak.

"Man, I just don't get it. As soon as a man thinks he knows a woman, she turns around and prove that he knows nothing at fuckin' all. You women are so damn confused. You ask for a good man, but when you get one, you fuck him over for the nigga who fucked over you." Sebastian's angered returned. Satin didn't speak, she just listened to him vent. "I'm sorry, but you really shouldn't be here right now. I really don't want to take my anger and frustration out on you. I mean… you came to see about me. I really didn't know you cared that much. I see you at work, but you hardly say anything to me."

At a loss for words and not sure how to respond to a man who was angry with women, Satin carefully chose her words. "Umm… you're right, I shouldn't be here, but I'm not sorry that I came. I'm really glad to see that you are okay."

Sebastian quickly stood up and it startled Satin.

"Do I look okay? Do I really fucking look okay?! You know nothing about me or nothing about what I'm going through to assume that I'm okay. I'M FUCKED UP! You hear me, FUCKED UP! The woman that I loved and dedicated four years of my FUCKING life trying to please, left me. She left me!" Sebastian sat back on the bed and a couple of tears filled his face.

Satin didn't know if she still should leave Sebastian alone at that point, or stay and offer comfort to a man she barely knew anything about, other than the fact that they work in the same building.

Satin walked over to Sebastian and placed her hand on his chin and slowly raised his face up to her. Her lace white bra showed through her wet white button up shirt. Sebastian noticed how attractive Satin was. A woman he barely noticed at work, but who was there in his home trying to comfort him.

Sebastian slowly stood to his feet. He was taller than Satin and looked down at her. "Like I said, I didn't know you cared so much," he reiterated.

Oh goodness, this is not supposed to be going this way. "I um… I didn't know I did either. I figured this was the least I could do. You did choose to invite me to your wedding; although we don't know each other personally."

"I did, didn't I?" Sebastian pulled Satin closer to him.

He moved in and slowly placed his lips on Satin's. Satin's innocent round eyes widened. She didn't reject him, but was feeling conflicted and confused about what was starting to happen between the two of them.

Satin knew Sebastian was emotionally wounded and wanted to show him comfort, but she knew his heart was with his ex, and hers was with the father of her child. The two of them begin to exchange saliva. Sebastian picked Satin up and she clasped her legs around him. He laid her down on the bed and begin to unbutton her wet blouse. Satin knew she should stop Sebastian, but she didn't. Something deep down inside of her wouldn't let her.

Satin then heard Bishop's voice, calling her promiscuous and full of sin. "No, no, no... I can't do this. Um... this is not why I came over here. I came to make sure you were okay and now that I know you are, I have to go, Sebastian."

Satin raised up from the bed and begun to button her shirt back up. Sebastian raised up and stood from the bed. "You're right, you should leave. Go now before I change my mind," Sebastian spoke firmly.

Sebastian was confused. He was hurt and wanted to ease his pain the quickest and best way he could. Looking at Satin and her breasts through a wet shirt turned his manhood on. Sebastian was thinking with his dick and not his head or heart. Any form of good feeling felt better than the true pain that was aching deep inside of him. Sebastian's injured heart just wouldn't stop bleeding and he was willing to settle for anything that would Band-Aid his emotions.

Satin wasn't thinking at all. It was who she was, living in the moment and having to deal with the consequences later.

"Okay." Satin begun to walk out of Sebastian's room. She stopped and turned around. "Hey, before I go, I ordered you some food. Be sure to listen for the delivery guy."

"Thank you, that's very nice of you to do that. How much do I owe you?"

"No problem, and you don't owe me anything. I, um… I'm not the one that should be giving any relationship advice, but…"

Sebastian interrupted yet again. "Then don't," he spoke with a serious look on his face.

"Oookay. I was just going to say everything will find a way to work itself out; that's it. Hey…you're not going to um… you know… do anything that might…"

Sebastian's interruption game was strong. He hardly let Satin finish any of her sentences.

"Kill myself? If I was going to kill myself, I would be dead already," he replied in a sarcastic manner.

Satin just stared and turned around to walk away.

"Hey!" Sebastian boomed.

Satin turned back around at the entrance of the bedroom door facing Sebastian.

Why are you starting to look so attractive to me? "Yes?"

"Thanks for stopping by, that's very considerate of you. I wish I was that considerate. After all you've done for me today, the least I could do is offer you a dry shirt. I have plenty like the one you have on, just in a man's version. You are more than welcome to one."

Satin smiled. "It's okay, it's almost dry now. I'll have to change it anyway once I get home and shower, properly that is, with my clothes off."

Damn did I just say that? I was so not trying to flirt with you or was I? Damn, now I'm all confused. Let me get my butt out of here.

"Now I have a visual," Sebastian teased.

Satin continued to smirk as she turned around and walked out of Sebastian's bedroom. She powerwalked down the stairs and out of Sebastian's loft. She jogged to her car and hopped in.

"WHAT THE HELL WAS THAT?!"

*****

A couple of days had passed and Satin was at home. Her and Nolan were not speaking to one another after he stayed out of the house two nights in a row and came rolling in at six o'clock in the morning just in enough time to get ready for work.

Satin was beginning to get fed up with Nolan's immature behavior. He didn't spend any time with her and barely any father bonding time with his own son. Satin was beginning to question her decision about asking him to move in with her so they could be a family and raise their child together.

Nolan was in the streets, and hitting them hard. The last thing on his mind was settling down with one woman and raising a child. Nolan convinced himself that he was doing the right thing by just living there at the apartment. He believed it would benefit Noah just by him staying there and the fact that Noah knew that he was his Daddy was enough.

Nolan never contemplated the energy it would take to raise a child, or that even spending quality time with one was crucial to a child's development. Nolan didn't know his own dad and he grew up believing that daddies were not needed because his momma was his mother and father and raised him all on her own. He figured Satin had that part under control.

Satin had other plans for herself, Nolan and Noah. She wanted to get married and stop living in sin. Although in the back of her mind, Satin couldn't help but think how much it would please her parents, especially Bishop.

"So how long are we going to do this?" Satin asked as she laid in the bed.

"This is all your doing, not mine. I'm good. You're the one who chose to stop talking to me."

"The things I want to talk about, you seemed to have no interest in, Nolan."

"I don't, and I'm not going to keep stressing that. Listen, you knew what it was before I came here. You asked me to move in to be here for my son. You never said anything about getting married. I ain't ready for no shit like that. You always got some shit with you, boy I tell you."

"But you were ready to put a baby inside of me," Satin sassed as she sat up.

"No, I wanted to fuck and we did; don't get it twisted. I don't regret the fact that Noah is here, but it's too late for all that shit now anyway. I told you, I ain't 'bout to let you or any other broad pressure me to do something I don't want to do. I'm twenty-one years old, man. I have my whole life ahead of me and I keep telling you, being married is not a good look for me."

"Well, how long do you expect me to just keep allowing you to stroll up in here any time you feel good and ready?"

"Let me? The fuck I look like to you, my son? You ain't got to *let me* do shit. I'm my own man. I do as I please, when I please," Nolan rumbled, full of himself.

"And a man doesn't disrespect his lady nor where he lies his head."

"You know what, this conversation is done, man. You are beginning to sound just like my fucking momma. I can go back home for all this bullshit."

Satin stopped talking. The last thing she wanted Nolan to do was leave. She ate the rest of her words, along with her pride and dropped the conversation; at least the part about him staying out all night. Deep down, Satin knew if Nolan had it easy at home with his momma, she would not have ever been able to convince him to move in with her. His mother's pressure about church forced him to leave home and she didn't want to do the same thing about marriage.

"Well, can I ask you one last thing?"

"What is it, Satin? It's too damn early to be bugging, yo. Nigga gotta go to work and listen to the white man on my back all day, and before I leave for work, I have to deal with this shit? What chu want, man?"

Nolan had begun to get frustrated with Satin and her antics to try and get him to marry her.

"I just really need to know whether you see marrying me and being a real family with me and our son somewhere down the line?"

Nolan didn't allow Satin's question to sink in before he bolted with an answer. His mind was made up and there was no changing it. "Honestly, I don't think that far ahead. Niggas dying left and right every day. I live for today, but since you asked, I don't know. I guess... only time will tell and I ain't in no rush. For the record, Noah is, and will always be, my real family."

Satin stared at Nolan. She noticed that Nolan had said Noah was and would always be his family, but he had not mentioned her as part of his family. She was beginning to wonder what she ever saw in him in the first place that had captured her attention and her heart. Noah's bad boy persona was no longer a challenge for her shy, preacher's kid personality. Opposites were no longer attracting. Satin was thinking about her future and the future of her child.

Nolan grabbed his hard hat and walked out the door. He felt no remorse from his response and hoped that Satin would just stop bugging him about marrying her all together. Nolan was content with living the life he had chosen, and wasn't about to let Satin detour his plans with the nagging. He went about his day and didn't even return straight home after he got off from work yet again. Nolan made every stop to everywhere else but home.

Satin and Noah spent their day inside. Noah was playing with his toys. Satin was content with watching her pride and joy when her phone rang.

"Hello?"

"What really happened that day at Sebastian's? I still feel that you are holding back."

What the hell? I know he better not be running his mouth.

"What are you talking about, Brandy?"

"Don't play coy with me, church girl. You know exactly what I'm talking about. What happened between the two of you?"

"Umm… nothing happened between the two of you, I mean two of us. Why do you ask?"

"I'm your bestie and I need to know these things. So, if nothing happened, why did Mr. Good looking just ask me for your number?"

"HE DID? I mean… he did?" Satin calmed her excitement down.

"Yes, as a matter of fact, he did. He *just* did!"

"So, that means he's back at work then?" Satin questioned as she allowed herself to be happy that Sebastian was good enough to finally return to work.

"Obviously."

"So, did you give it to him?" Satin probed.

"Did you want me to give it to him? Did you give *it* to him?" Brandy teased as if she knew there was more to the story, and had every intention on dragging it out of Satin.

Brandy didn't know much about Satin other than Satin telling her she was raised in the church and that her father was a pastor. Satin intentionally left her struggles out of the conversation. Brandy also knew of Nolan. Nothing personal, just that he was Satin's boyfriend and son's father.

"If I would have given *it* to him, he wouldn't be asking you for it, now would he? And besides, I guess he just wants to thank me for stopping by. I'm sure that's it."

"I wasn't talking about you giving him your number, and um… if you say so, P.K."

Talk that shit, but I know how y'all get down.

"Brandy… if you don't get your doggone mind out of the gutter. I told you, nothing happened. I went over to check on the dude. I found that he was okay… well not totally okay because he had been drinking, but very much so alive and I left. THAT WAS IT," Satin stressed.

"Yeah, keep singing that same tune to the choir, but we all know better."

"Believe what you will, heathen, but I've already told you *several* times, nothing happened," Satin teased.

"Proudly, but any who… Yes, I gave the accountant your number. Was it okay that I did?" Brandy questioned as she searched for any indication that Satin was excited about Sebastian having her number.

"Umm… I guess it's okay. Like I've said, I'm sure he just wants to thank me."

"For a service, well rendered *orrrr*…" Brandy kept her insinuating that they'd slept together going.

"Thanks for calling and informing me, bye Brandy." Satin hung up the phone and smiled to herself.

Why am I even getting a least bit excited that he asked for my number? The man is obviously still in love with his ex, he can't possibly be interested in me. Damn... that kiss though. Now I need to get my thoughts out the gutter. I'm glad that he has returned to work, though. Good for him.

Satin's phone vibrated indicating she had a text.

BRANDY: *If u wouldn't have hung up on me, I would have told you that the bank got robbed.*

SATIN: *WHAT?!!! Where you there when it happened? Did any1 get hurt?*

BRANDY: *Yes, I was here, but at lunch. No 1 got hurt but a lot of loot was stolen. They are questioning EVERYONE. U may be next.*

SATIN: *Wow... that's crazy! Glad ur ok.*

BRANDY: *Yeah, I'm good. I'll call u later 2 tell you more. The General has been riding her broom even harder ever since. Be grateful ur suspended!*

SATIN: *lol, I can only imagine! Call me later!*

BRANDY: *Later babes!*

Maybe that's why Sebastian wanted my number. I guess he'll be the one doing the questioning. Well, I'll be damned.

Chapter Eleven
A Simple Thank You
Goes a Long Ways

The next day, Satin filled out several applications online.

She was a mother on a mission and didn't have time to wait around to be dismissed from her current job. Satin wasn't completely convinced that her job's security was stable at the bank after the last conversation she had with Janice. Not to mention, the recent robbery didn't make her feel safe.

Satin didn't feel secure with Nolan sticking around after he chose to dismiss her concerns about staying out all night, or even the possibility of marrying her one day. Satin was feeling pressure, and she knew she needed to do something, and do something quick. Depending on her parents was not a luxury she could afford and she had Noah to think about.

Hardships taught Satin that she was in control of her own destiny. Satin was very fearful of possibly ending up at the women's shelter with Noah. It was a place that she didn't look down on, but it was definitely where she didn't want to return to as a house guest.

Satin updated her resume and sent out several copies to different companies. She was desperate and didn't put much thought into what kind of job she wanted. Right now, anything to keep a roof over her and Noah's head was good enough.

After spending, most of her morning job hunting, Satin also cooked, washed clothes and cleaned her apartment. Before she knew it, the time had quickly passed and it was well after six in the evening. There was no sign of Nolan again after work.

Satin had prepared mashed potatoes, Salisbury steaks and vegetables in hopes of the three of them sitting down and having dinner. She called Nolan's phone, but he did not answer. She then decided to call her mother after not speaking to her for a few days.

"Hi, Ma, how are you?"

"Hey baby, I'm doing a bit better since the last time we spoke," Carolyn lied. "How are you and the baby?"

"Oh, we're fine. I found Noah a sitter for the time being, but we're good. You know, I would have come to see you if it had not been for Bishop…"

Carolyn interrupted, "Not today, sweetheart, not today. Momma just don't feel like getting into all of that today, but I'm glad you've found someone to tend to Noah. I hate that I couldn't continue to keep him, but… it's like I said, I really don't want to get into all of that today."

"We really don't have to Ma, okay? I just wanted to hear your voice, that's why I called you," Satin spoke calmly. She didn't want to upset her mother and decided not to go in on Bishop yet again.

"Thanks baby, thanks for calling. You know I love you and there's nothing in the world I wouldn't do for you. I love my grandson too, very much."

Except not enough to defy your husband. "I know Ma, and Noah and I love you too."

"I'll come see the both of you soon, okay?" Carolyn promised.

"Are you sure you're okay, Ma? You don't sound like yourself. You sound a bit down." Satin noticed the change in her mother's tone. Initially, Satin believed it was because of her talking about her daddy, but Satin sensed there was something more. Carolyn just didn't sound like herself at all and it wasn't the norm for her. She had an uplifting personality and Satin could always count on Carolyn for enthusiasm.

"No, baby, I'm fine. I was napping right before you called. Maybe that's why I sound the way that I do."

"Oh okay. And Bishop, is he there with you?"

"Yes, your father is here with me. He's in his study. We have bible study in a few hours, and that's why I was napping, so I can be alert for the Lord and open to receive his word."

That's right, bible study is tonight. I surely haven't been to one of them in a good minute. "Amen. I'm just checking, I was beginning to worry about you."

"I know baby, but there's no need to worry about me, I'm okay. I've already seen a doctor after not feeling well the other day, and she said my pressure was just a bit elevated, and I needed to watch my stress levels. I've been really trying hard not to let anything get to me, and I have started to feel a bit better. I checked my pressure today and it was pretty good."

"That's good to know, Ma. I'm glad you're doing better, and please do come by and see us soon. I miss you, and I'm sure Noah misses his grandma, too."

"Aww…" Carolyn chuckled. "I surely miss the two of you as well. I'm about to finish my cat nap and I'll talk to later, baby."

"Okay, Ma. I love you."

"I love you more."

Satin and Carolyn ended their call.

Satin wished things were different between her and her family, but things always remained the same. A tear fell from her eyes when she thought of her mother feeling ill and she couldn't go to see about her. Satin remembered Carolyn getting off the phone with her because she said she was exhausted on their prior call, but she didn't know that her mother's pressure was acting up. Satin cherished Carolyn and the piece of relationship that they've managed to keep due to the circumstances.

Satin's phone rung, interrupting her thoughts. She didn't recognize the number, but she answered it anyway.

"Satin?"

"Yes?"

"Hi, this is Sebastian. I hope you don't mind me calling you, are you busy now?" Sebastian's deep tone resonated through the phone.

"Uh... no, I'm not busy. How are you, Sebastian? I heard you returned to work. That's very good to know."

"Yeah, I did. I wish I could say I'm glad to be back but hey, it could be worse, right?"

"Right."

"So, Satin, I just wanted to thank you again for what you did for me the other day. I don't remember everything, due to my condition and all." He slightly laughed. "But aye... I just wanted to apologize for my rudeness. Man, you were only trying to help and I was rude."

"No apologies needed, I totally understood. You are going through something."

"Yes, I am, but it doesn't give me an excuse to behave the way that I did. I'm very sorry for touching you inappropriately. That wasn't my intentions, and especially not towards someone who was only there to try and help me."

So, you didn't enjoy the kiss? "Like I said, no apologies needed, I understand. And besides, I totally forgot all about it."

Stop lying, you think about that kiss more than you should.

"Well in that case, that makes two of us. Listen… did you have dinner already?"

"Dinner?" Satin looked over at the pots on the stove. "Uh no, I didn't have dinner yet," she lied.

My butt going straight to hell. Why did I just lie to this man?

"Good. I just ordered some take out from BJ's. It's a really good place over there on Centennial Center. It hasn't arrived yet though; you should come have dinner with me. I mean, that's the least I can do is share my take-out with you."

Oh, he sounds so mature. What a man! "Dinner? I don't know…"

"Listen… not like a dinner date, more like friends hanging out. You know… since you're visit to my place, I sort of kind of feel like we are friends now. Well to be perfectly honest, I don't have many friends, and the few I do have are trying to throw women at me and take me to the strip clubs as if a damn stripper can cure my broken heart. The only thing I have interest in right now is work and piecing my life back together. That's it. My strip club days have been over with. I leave that to them youngsters who don't have anything better to do with their cash but give it away to a woman for a five-minute thrill. Naw, they can have that."

Satin smiled on the inside.

I love the way you think. "Dinner, that's it?"

"Yes, dinner and chill, but I don't mean that Netflix and chill shit either."

Satin tittered. "Okay, dinner and chill it is then, but give me about thirty minutes and I'll hit you back to let you know if I'm on my way or not."

"You not blowing me off, are you?" Sebastian teased.

"Naw, nothing like that. It's just that I have my son and I need to ask his babysitter if she would keep him while I come over. I can't say yes for certain until I can be certain I have a babysitter."

"You have a son? How old is he?"

"Yes, I do, and he's three."

"Oh wow, a son, that's cool. I always wanted kids and especially a son. Hey, why don't you bring him along? We all can have dinner together and that way you can really know that I meant dinner and chill."

Wow… this man wants to have dinner with my son and hasn't even met him, while his stupid daddy won't even bother; he's a sad excuse for a damn father.

"That's very kind of you to invite Noah, but not this time, maybe next time."

"Okay, whatever you want to do it's totally up to you; just know that he's welcome."

"Thanks, I appreciate that."

More than you know.

"No problem. So, go on and do what you gotta do and hit me back."

"Will do. See you soon, hopefully anyway," Satin smiled.

"Yeah, hopefully. Later," Sebastian ended the call.

"Come here, baby." Satin reached out to Noah. She picked him up and placed Noah on her hip. "How would you like it if I took you to see Mrs. Karen?"

"Mee-maw?"

"Is Mrs. Karen your Mee-maw now?" *You must get that from her grandson.*

"Yes, Mee-maw."

"Well do you want to spend time with Mee-maw today?"

"Yay… Mee-maw, Mommy, I want to see Mee-maw."

"Okay, my love bug, I'll take you to see Mee-maw. I will put you in your bed so Mommy can shower, and then we are going to see Mee-maw, okay?"

"Okay, Mommy," Noah answered in his delicate tone.

Satin placed Noah inside of his bed with all his favorite toys and she stepped inside the bathroom to take a quick shower. She thought about Sebastian inviting Noah, and how cool of a guy he had to be to want to be bothered with a three-year-old child that wasn't his.

Satin was starting to like Sebastian, far more than she was willing to admit to herself. She saw a wounded man, but also a man with a kind heart who was just trying to figure out how to heal his broken heart as anyone would have in his position.

Satin knew that she didn't want to try and start anything with Sebastian, other than what the two of them had already started in his bedroom. She knew Sebastian wasn't by any means ready to move on that quickly, and she convinced herself that there wasn't nothing wrong with getting to know him better outside the workplace good mornings they exchanged with one another.

Satin slipped into a little black dress that stopped right above her knee caps. She slipped into her favorite comfortable black ballerina shoes, grabbed Noah and out the door she went. Satin wasn't big on heavy make-up, but her sophisticated arched eyebrows harmonized her oval face perfectly. Satin's naturally tanned skin didn't need any powder and paint; it glowed all on it's on. Her effortlessly curly silk tresses fell to her shoulders. Satin was all natural, except for a little clear gloss she dabbed on her heart shaped lips.

Satin held Noah's hand and knocked on Karen's door. "I'm sorry to bother you Mrs. Karen, are you busy?"

"Hey Sugah, and no I'm not busy, come on in," Karen responded as she moved to the side and let Satin and Noah in.

"Hey, Mee-maw's sweet Noah. I haven't seen you in a couple of days. Have you forgotten about Mee-maw already?"

Karen picked Noah up and held him. She kissed him on the cheek and rubbed his head. Noah hugged her tight and smiled.

"Mrs. Karen, I know I don't have the right to ask this of you, but I really need a favor."

"What is it, sweetheart? Go on, just ask what you need to ask."

"Umm… I know I haven't paid you yet for the one day that you kept Noah, and I know it's after babysitting hours, but um…. I was wondering would you keep Noah for me just for a couple of hours? I promise to be back no later than eight thirty or nine for certain."

"Sure, you know I don't mind keeping my sweet Noah. About that one day, I told you when you came to get Noah and you told me you were suspended for this week that you didn't have to pay me. Child, it was only one day."

"Yes, I know, but I still was going to pay you anyway. I just felt bad about not paying you after you watched him. I look at it this way, I have to pay the day care whether Noah misses a day or not."

"Well, I'm not the day care. I'm Mee-maw, ain't that right, my sweet Noah?"

Karen looked at Noah and his face lit up in pure joy to be back at Karen's house where all the snacks were.

"Oh Mrs. Karen thank you so much, I really appreciate you."

"No problem, honey. I told you when God gives you a blessing, take it. It's yours to have."

Satin leaned in and hugged Karen tightly. She kissed her on the cheek. "I love you, Mrs. Karen. Noah loves you, too," Satin said as her eyes teared up from thinking about the nice lady who was always eager to help her out.

"Aww... I love you guys too. Look at it this way, you and Noah are now my extended family. My newfound daughter and beautiful grandbaby, if that's okay with you?"

"Absolutely, it's okay with me, you are a great woman and I inspire to be just like you when I grow up."

"And you will. I know you won't let all this goodness go to waste. You must pay it forward in this life."

"Absolutely, I agree," Satin smiled.

"Now, where are you going all dressed up?"

"Dressed up? Oh, this old thing. It's just something I pulled out of the closet."

A dress I got from Wal-Mart.

"Well, you surely look mighty fancy to me. Are you and Noah's dad going out?" Karen questioned out of pure curiosity. She had no reason to think Satin was going visit another man. All she knew was what she saw which was Nolan at Satin's apartment.

Aw man Mrs. Karen, why did you have to ask that? I can't even lie to you.

"No, Noah's dad is not home. I'm going visit a friend."

"Oh... I see. Well, this old lady will mind her own business," Karen spoke and Satin smiled. "I'll just take it as you know what you're doing, and if I were you, I would be careful. Don't think about starting something elsewhere if you have unfinished business at home. Do you know what I mean?"

"Yes, Ma'am. I know exactly what you mean. I'll just say this, and then we can really talk about something else, Noah's father and I are not married. Just yesterday, he basically told me that he didn't have plans on ever marrying me. The person I'm going to visit is just a friend, really Mrs. Karen. I helped him out, I guess you can say, and he just wants to share dinner with me; that's it. Nothing else but dinner and time spent with a friend," Satin smiled.

"You don't owe me no explanation as to what you're doing or who you're doing it with. I should have just kept my big mouth closed."

"No Ma'am, I'm glad you said something. I have nothing to hide, and besides, I really respect and value your opinion. So, thank you."

"Okay, my baby, go on, have fun."

Satin smiled. She leaned in and kissed Noah. "See you in a little while, okay son?"

"Bye, Mommy."

"Oh, yeah... Mrs. Karen, Noah shouldn't be hungry. I've already fed and bathed him. He'll probably drift off to sleep in a minute."

"Okay, if he does, I'll lay him in the playpen. See you when you get back."

"Okay," Satin said and walked out of the door.

Chapter Twelve

What May Come of a Broken Heart

Satin took a slow drive to Sebastian's place. She thought about everything Karen said and took it into consideration. She convinced herself that she wasn't trying to start anything with Sebastian, but also admitted to herself that she was indeed attracted to him. Sebastian was young, successful in his career and appeared to have a kind heart. He scored major brownie points with Satin for inviting Noah to spend the evening with them. Any young woman in her right mind would have been lucky to have Sebastian as her man. Unfortunately for Angela, another woman would benefit from all the love he wanted to give to her.

Satin never thought in her wildest dream that a man could be that sincere towards her son because her own father rejected him. Sebastian's kind gesture may have just been that, a kind gesture, but to Satin it was everything because Noah didn't have a father or grandfather who was enthused about spending an evening with him. A tear escaped Satin's eyes as she thought about her son and the example of a man Noah didn't have in his life.

Satin looked at her phone to see if Nolan decided to return any of her calls or even send a text message. Her phone was dry, not a voicemail or text from anyone. It angered Satin that Nolan was unconcerned about her and how she felt. Satin started to think that Nolan didn't care enough about Noah either. If he did, he would have returned the calls.

Satin silently prayed to God to help her make better choices for herself and for Noah. She told God that she didn't sign up to be a single parent, but unfortunately for Noah, she was one anyway.

Satin finally pulled up to Sebastian's loft and parked in the driveway. She glanced in the mirror and finger rolled the out of place curls, then she reached in her purse and grabbed the lip gloss. Satin swiped her lips a few times, then matted them together to even the gloss across. She placed the gloss back inside her purse, along with the cell phone and keys. Satin opened the door and walked to the front door.

She rang the doorbell and Sebastian opened the door within seconds. He was relaxed in a fitted black T-shirt and blue jeans, but was barefoot. Satin glanced down at his feet and smiled. Sebastian's eyes shadowed hers and he noticed that Satin was eyeing his feet.

"My bad, I always walk around here barefoot and naked, but I'm sure you know that already," Sebastian spoke, reflecting on the day that Satin was at his home.

"Ah yeah, I noticed that the other day," Satin continued to leer.

"That's right, you're the nice young lady that helped my drunken ass with a shower?"

Satin lightly chuckled. "Yes, I guess that would be me. I would be that lady."

"Hey, I'm glad you could make it, come on in," Sebastian said as he stepped aside and let Satin through the door. "Why didn't you call me and let me know that you were outside? I would have come out and opened the door for you."

Oh wow…really? A gentleman indeed.

"That's okay, I'm good," Satin answered as the smile on her face matched the smile on her insides.

"Oh, believe me, I know you're good with your cute lil self, but let me know next time so I can get that for you," Sebastian flirted.

Satin blushed. "Yes, sir, will do," she teased.

"Do you mind if we eat in the theater room? I was watching the game, but we don't have to if you don't want to."

"Uh sure, that's fine with me," Satin answered. She was happy to be back at Sebastian's, sharing dinner with him. It did not matter to her one way or another where they ate. Every spot in Sebastian's place was inviting through Satin's eyes.

"Okay, cool. I'll just grab the food from the kitchen and take it up. By the way, you look nice," Sebastian flirted again.

"Thank you. I would say you do too, but your feet are a major distraction," Satin joked.

"Ohhhh... so you ragging a nigga's feet? Girl, I told you, I walk around here butt ass naked, so be happy I put some clothes on just for you, *or* I can always just take them off. I mean, you pretty much saw my ass already," Sebastian kidded.

"No, no, please keep them on," Satin tittered.

"You're too easy, I'm just messing with you. I wouldn't do you that. I'm sure you saw enough of my nakedness for one day already."

How can I forget? I can't get the image out of my head if I wanted to, and I don't think I do.

Satin grinned to herself.

Sebastian grabbed the take-out bag and his beer. "Hey, why don't you grab our dinnerware off the counter? I would grab it myself, but as you can see, my hands are pretty tied up. Do you want a beer?"

"No, I'm good," Satin answered as she grabbed the all-white square cut dinner plates off the counter, along with two silver forks.

"Do you prefer wine instead?"

"I'm sorry, I should have just said I don't drink. I'll take a water, though."

"My bad, love, why didn't you just say so? I was about to say, don't go getting all shy on me now. You saw me at my absolute worst, you got the ups on me because I don't know anything about you," Sebastian teased and Satin tittered in an adorable tone.

Sebastian led the way up the stairs into the theater room. He took a seat in the red leather recliner and Satin sat next to him in hers.

"Aw man, I was rushing to get back to the game, I wasn't thinking. We probably should have fixed the plates down stairs on the counter, then brought them up. I will make a complete mess.

"Give it to me, I'll fix them," Satin insisted as she sat the plates in her lap and reached her hands out for the bag of food.

"Are you sure? I mean, I can do mine and you just fix yours. I don't want to mess your plate up though, and that's why you should fix your own if you don't want a sloppy plate of food."

"It's okay, I'll take care of it. I got you," Satin winked.

Sebastian smiled and thought for a brief second. "Can I ask you something?"

"Sure," Satin answered as she set up to put the takeout onto their dinnerware.

"Are you really this kind, or are you just feeling sorry for me and being nice to me because I have a broken heart? Do you take care of everyone you meet in this way?"

Sebastian's in-depth questions caught Satin's attention. She finished transferring the food and handed him his plate. "It's really not a big deal, Sebastian. I just placed food you ordered for us onto another plate. Let's just say, I'm only good at it because I have to do this all the time with a three-year-old running around. My son hates sitting in his high chair to eat, so I'm transferring his food constantly," Satin answered.

Sebastian fixated his eyes on Satin with a serious stare as he observed her. "And the other day? What about all that you have done for me, and the fact that you didn't even know me outside of work? Hell, we never really said much to each other but good morning."

"Let's just say... do onto others as you want done onto you."

Sebastian was taken by Satin's humbleness and will to help others. "It's that simple?" he questioned.

"Pretty much, at least that's what I was taught."

Until my father changed the rules because I got pregnant at seventeen.

Smitten by Satin's personality, Sebastian realized he wanted to get to know as much about Satin that night as he possibly could. He wasn't over his ex, but quite thrilled that he had stumbled upon on a friendship by accident. Sebastian thought of Satin as a beautiful human who also just happened to possess a beautiful spirit and adorable smile.

"If you don't mind me asking, how old are you, Satin?"

"I'm uh… I'm twenty. Why do you ask?"

"I don't know; I guess it's called curiosity. But here's what I don't get, I don't understand your sense of compassion towards others and generosity at such a young age. Most people your age are selfish. They only think of themselves. I know I did at that age."

Satin smiled. She took in every nice compliment that her newfound friend offered. She wasn't completely sure the state of mind Sebastian was in, considering the obvious, but Satin was quite impressed with his kindness towards her.

"If you don't mind me asking, how old are you?" Satin returned the question.

"I'm twenty-eight. Yep, got you by eight, baby girl," Sebastian winked.

"I see. So, I gotta admit, you are surely doing a hell of lot better than the last time I was here."

Sebastian smiled and sat back. "You think? Looks could definitely be deceiving."

"Yeah, you're right, but you are in a better mood than the last time, for certain. You even look better, too," Satin teased, but once she realized she was coming on to Sebastian, she back doored. "I mean… more in a healthy kind of sort of way. You know what I mean?" Satin tried to clean up her come on remark.

"So, you're saying that I look better with my clothes on?"

"No no… I mean… I'm just saying your spirit seems to be lifted as opposed to last time."

"I told you, you're way too easy; I'm just messing with you, baby girl," Sebastian chuckled. "You will learn that about me. I joke a lot, but when I need to be serious, I am. There's no in between with me; hot or cold, that's it."

"Ohhh, that I do know."

"Damn, I was that bad the other day?"

"Yeah, kind of. You may have hurt my little feelings a bit. Just a tiny bit," Satin teased as she showed her fingers as an example of a little bit.

"Aw my bad, baby girl. Do you want me to get you a Band-Aid? I can get you one. And besides, that wasn't really me; that was that damn Remy and my wounded heart. Blame it on the alcohol," Sebastian teased.

Satin looked, rolled her eyes and a warm smile swept across her face. She was beginning to see that Sebastian was really a joker and a laid-back type of guy. Sebastian mouthed a full fork of his food and Satin began to eat hers as well. He told Satin he was watching the game, but since she'd been there, he hadn't looked once at the screen and the TV ended up watching them. Lost in each other's company, Sebastian and Satin continued to talk.

"But on some real shit, love, I am truly sorry for my rudeness. I should have never taken out on you what someone else did to me. That ain't cool at all."

"I told you, no apologies, I understand. But I must ask, how are you really, Sebastian? You said looks can be deceiving. You look fine, but you insinuate that you're not."

"Well, I am a man, I will bounce back *eventually*. I mean, don't get me wrong, my heart is broken, still broken, but I can't give up and besides, I'm all out of Remy Martin anyway."

Satin buttered at Sebastian's playful personality.

He continued, "But all jokes aside, all I have is one day at a time, you know what I mean? You being here is really helping me, more than you know. Listen, I know we barely know each other, and that's why I invited you over because I want to change that. Chilling with you has really taken my mind off what my heart feels. Maybe we should spend more time together, and really get to know each other better."

Satin's innocent eyes could not stop blinking. Sebastian had made her nervous.

"No no, relax, nothing like that, baby girl. What I meant was that you seem to be a very nice young lady. I never met anyone like you before, and especially someone who would have done what you done. That speaks a lot about your character and upbringing. I just hope, whoever the lucky dude is that you have in your life, appreciates the kind woman that you are because believe me… women like you are hard to come by, I should know. Somehow, you walked into my life and I like it, I like you. That's all I'm saying."

Satin observed Sebastian for a moment. She admired his strength, kindness and broken heart that was on its way to healing. She thought about how Sebastian was just emotionally broken down, damn near to nothing the other day, and there he was bouncing back and trying to move forward with his life one day at time. Satin didn't confirm nor deny that she had someone in her life, but agreed wholeheartedly with Sebastian. She had begun to feel something, other than empathy towards him; she had begun to like him, too.

Satin wondered why a woman would choose not to marry a guy like Sebastian when he appeared to be honest and sincere. She knew it wasn't a money issue, or needless to say, that he came up short in the sexually pleasing a woman department. Satin tried to read through what Sebastian was not saying, but she came up with nothing; he was rather transparent.

She finished her last piece of steak and potato, and wiped her mouth with the napkin.

"Sebastian, may I ask you something?"

"Shoot."

"You are a successful, intelligent strong man. You appear to be nice and caring from what I can see. Why do you think your fiancée changed her mind about getting married?"

"Damn… you don't beat around the bush, do you? Somebody came for answers."

"You said I could ask, so I did," Satin shrugged her shoulders.

"You right, you right… I did," Sebastian uttered as he stuck his fork into his last piece of steak and put it in his mouth. He chewed it up and chased it down with Heineken. Sebastian made a sucking noise with his teeth, removing the excess meat, and set the plate underneath his seat and got comfortable in the chair.

"You know… the signs were always there, but I loved her so much, and still do love her. Stupidly, I chose to ignore them. I figured… if I would show all the love that she desperately needed, she would see that I loved and respected her far more than he ever did or ever could. I showered that woman with love, gifts and I even purchased this place because she saw it and fell in love. I'm from the hood, I could live anywhere and be okay. Maybe not anywhere, but you know what I mean."

Satin smiled. "Yeah, I know what you mean."

"She wanted a place in the suburbs, I purchased a place for us in the suburbs. She wanted a three-carat diamond ring, I bought her a three-carat diamond. She wanted liposuction before the wedding because she worried that she wouldn't look good in her dress without it. So, what do I do, I paid for her to have liposuction, although I thought she was good without it. I mean… that's just to name a few things. She didn't have to ask for my time or attention, it was always there constantly. I didn't skip a beat; I know I didn't. I made damn sure not to because I knew she was one of those women who feigned and got off on a man complimenting her. So, to answer your question, my love wasn't enough. She was still in love with her ex. The pussy ass nigga who beat her ass and left her for dead."

Satin's mouth dropped open. "You mean to tell me she left you for a man who tried to kill her?"

"Yep, life a bitch, ain't it?"

"Wow, that's crazy."

"No, it's not. Life is what you make of it. I know I said it was a bitch, but it meant that in a way of a dog. People dogging each other out. When I met that woman, she was at her lowest point. She was timid, had nothing, scared to love and just knew that I was a woman beater like her ex. It took me damn near our entire relationship to convince her that I was nothing like him, and that every man doesn't beat women, but I guess that's wasn't enough. I guess I wasn't toxic and some people thrive off that shit; toxic love."

"Well, I don't think love is supposed to be toxic. I believe it should heal people instead."

"I knew there was a reason why I liked you. Not only are your kind, but you're pretty smart and wise for a twenty-year-old."

"Wise? Naw, I wouldn't say I'm wise at all. A little experienced, maybe, but that's only because life has taught me a thing or two."

"Interesting... since you already know so much about me, tell me about you? What exactly life has taught you? You're only twenty. What could you have possibly experienced that has made you wiser than most your age?" Sebastian inquired.

"And here I thought we were having a good conversation. So... what team are you rooting for?"

Satin tried to change the story because she didn't want to get into her experiencing homelessness and pregnancy at such a young age. Satin dreaded the fact that she had not reconciled with her father, but Sebastian thought she was a kind person because he didn't know of the resentment for her own father she harbored. Satin didn't want Sebastian to think less of her. She had gotten enough of that from Bishop and Nolan already. With Sebastian, it was a clean slate for Satin, and she wanted to keep it that way.

"Oh, it's like that, aye? Sooner or later, you will let me in. Just know, that's how two people get to know each other. Imma leave it alone for now, but one day soon, I would like to continue this conversation, baby girl."

Satin knew she wasn't being fair, but she wasn't ready to bare her soul. "Okay."

Sebastian let his curiosity go and glanced at the TV for the first time since Satin had arrived at his place. "I'm riding with Curry; all day, every day. That dude is talented," Sebastian teased.

Satin smiled and continued to ask Sebastian questions about the basketball game. They enjoyed each other's company and talked about work related stuff. Sebastian told Satin that he looked for her when he returned to work, and Satin gave him her version of why she was suspended. He encouraged Satin to hang in there at the bank, and focus less on her boss's attitude and more on what she was there to do; serve the customers.

Satin tried to give Sebastian her excuses as to why she was looking for another job, but he wasn't buying them. He expressed to Satin that excuses got him nowhere in life, and she needed to not give up so easily. Sebastian tried to convince Satin she could have a career at the bank, and not just a job. The opportunities were limitless and she needed to get on board.

Satin wasn't completely pleased with Sebastian's straight forwardness about what was best for her, but she respected his mind. The two of them ended their evening on a good note and Satin returned home at the time she had promised Karen. She picked up Noah and went into her apartment. Nolan was sitting on the couch and was pissed off to the max that she was not there when he got home.

Chapter Thirteen

Ain't No Fun When the Rabbit Got the Gun

"Man, where the fuck you been? I been sitting here waiting for you to come home!" Nolan thundered as soon as Satin's feet stepped inside of the apartment.

No, you're not getting mad because I wasn't home after not answering your phone.

"You would have known where I was, Nolan, had you answered any of my calls. And I would really appreciate if you lower your tone, you are going to wake my baby."

Nolan abruptly rose from the sofa. He reached his arms out and placed them underneath Noah's rested arms. "Fuck what you talkin' 'bout, give me my son, this is my son!" Nolan continued to roar as he took Noah out of Satin's arm, carried him to the bedroom and laid him down. Noah was sound asleep, and hadn't heard a thing.

Satin took a seat on the sofa and shook her head. She didn't want to go into the bedroom because she did not feel like being bothered with Nolan and his unexpected attitude. Satin thought about Nolan's arrogance and how he had the audacity to question her about her whereabouts, but never answered any of her calls while he was out doing only God knew what. Nolan was a prime example of *wanting his cake and eating it too*. He dished it out, but could not take it.

Nolan walked back into the living room and hovered over Satin in front of the couch. With a wrinkled forehead, brutal eyes, tightened lips and suspicious thoughts in his head that would not stop, he became an angry man. The more Nolan had sat and waited for Satin to return, the angrier he became.

"Imma ask you one more time. Where the fuck you been, and dressed like that?"

This Wal-Mart dress really must be working its magic because everyone has something to say about it, even this fool is in his feelings. "Nolan, where were you? I've been calling you for damn near four hours, and you never returned any of my calls, but you have the nerve to question me about where I've been? I'm not stupid, Nolan, I know you're cheating on me."

Satin stood up and attempted to walk off. "You think this is a fucking game?" Nolan rumbled as he manhandled Satin, and threw her back down on the sofa.

Satin immediately recognized the switch in Nolan's behavior and was confused as to where it was coming from, considering the fact she had started to believe Nolan did not care enough about her.

Satin saw a devilish look in Nolan's eyes and became fearful. She attempted to scream but Nolan palmed her mouth with his hand, and smothered her words. "Shut the fuck up before you wake my son up. Where the fuck you been, huh? You been out fucking some nigga in that dress?" Nolan taunted as he continued to restrain Satin on the couch with his hands still masking her mouth.

Satin tried to wiggle her way from underneath Nolan, and somehow remove his hands from her mouth, but he was much stronger than she was. Satin's heart hurtled in her chest and she wasn't sure what Nolan would do in his state of emotion.

Nolan continued to suffocate Satin's scream with his palm. "I said shut the fuck up! You fucked some nigga, didn't you? You fucked the nigga?" Nolan questioned repeatedly.

Satin couldn't verbally respond, she shook her head no, in fear of not responding at all and was too afraid to chance Nolan completely losing it. Tears begun to fill Satin's eyes. She was now experiencing a side of Nolan that she didn't know existed until that night. Satin was always available to Nolan whenever he needed her to be. Nolan wasn't used to Satin not being home after nine o'clock at night, let alone out in the street somewhere while he had no idea as to where. Nolan wanted his cake and to eat it too. He wanted to do what he wanted to do, but when Satin wasn't home waiting for him, he lost all control.

Nolan continued to pin Satin down with one hand, and with the other, he unbuttoned his pants, and allowed them to fall as he pushed his boxers down with them. Nolan pried Satin's legs apart as she struggled to keep them closed. Satin struggled and fought with Nolan as much as she could, but with hands over her mouth and being restrained on her back, there was little she could do; she felt trapped.

"Open your motherfucking legs! You said you ain't been with no nigga. Well, there's only one way to find out." Nolan roughly inserted himself inside of Satin. He plunged and forced as Satin's eyes peered upward to the ceiling. Satin begun to slip into a trance; she couldn't believe what Nolan was doing to her.

Satin thought about the conversation her and Sebastian had about his ex, and she begun to feel like the toxic woman Sebastian spoke about. Satin felt battered, and didn't have a clue as to what she was going to do about the father of her child assaulting and raping her. Tears dashed down Satin's face as she was reminded of an incident she tried to bury in her head that had happened when she was homeless. Mental notes resurfaced of the betrayer's face, and flashed back and forth across her mind. That wasn't the first-time Satin had been assaulted by a man, and the feeling of a man she knew raping her was no different from the attack of stranger. Satin was violated once again and bore great trouble in her mind, body and soul.

Nolan ignored Satin's tears and continued to pound on top of her like a dog in heat. Not long after he was done and egotistically unapologetic, Nolan pulled his pants up and went to wash off his malicious doing in the shower. He then got in the bed with a cold heart, and an empty conscious. Satin never moved from the couch. She wasn't physically or emotionally able. She slept with her eyes wide shut.

*****

After not leaving the apartment for two days, and mentally beating herself up, Satin finally forgave herself for what happened and convinced herself that she was okay. Sebastian texted a couple of times, but Satin didn't reply; she was embarrassed and humiliated. Satin's self-esteem was shattered, and she didn't want to confront anyone.

Nolan took a lot from Satin that night. Not only did he steal her joy, peace and body, Nolan stole her dignity as well. Satin felt alone and as though she didn't have anyone to confide in who would understand. She knew Karen was available and could offer up some good, sound advice, but Satin was too embarrassed to admit that she was raped by the same man she mothered a child with, and the same man she shared an apartment with and wanted to marry.

Nolan, on the other hand, carried on like nothing ever happened. He went about his days and nights, which kept him hanging out all night as usual, as though everything was back to normal.

Nolan was not a least bit worried about Satin leaving again. He was proud that he scared her straight. He arrogantly believed that his strong arm put Satin in her proper place, following in the footsteps of other fools he ran with. Nolan witnessed his friends manhandling their ladies and figured it was what a man was supposed to do to control a woman. He didn't know how to lead by example because his own pappy didn't stick around long enough to teach him any better.

Nolan gloated at the deranged idea of him being the man. He felt that Satin should stay in her lane. Her rightful place was as a woman and that she should have not done as a man would have.

The week had passed and Monday morning quickly came. Satin was due to return to work. Noah was with Karen and Nolan was at work. Satin was looking forward to returning to her duties, but wasn't looking forward to facing Sebastian after not responding to any of his text. Satin thought long and hard about Sebastian's last text stating that he wasn't into forcing friendships that weren't wanted. He let her knew he enjoyed the short time that they spent together and wished Satin well in her endeavors. Sebastian also advised Satin to think about what he told her about building a career at the bank and not letting Janice dictate her possibilities.

Satin didn't want her new platonic friendship with Sebastian to be over, but felt as though Nolan would spaz out if he found out about it. She didn't want to endure the agony of feeling empty again, as she felt as though her soul had left its temple that unforgettable night. Satin knew deep down inside that Nolan was not the man for her, but she was torn between what she thought was best for Noah and what was best for herself.

Satin made the ultimate sacrifice as youngest mothers did and decided to do what she believed was best for Noah, which was keeping his daddy in his life by any means necessary, but that didn't mean that she made the right choice.

Satin arrived to work twenty minutes early. She had processed everything Janice drilled before smacking her with a suspension. Janice's words penetrated Satin's mind, along with Sebastian's input about opportunities at the bank. Satin was determined to make an impressionable return if it killed her. The saying, 'the early bird gets the worm' was nothing new at the bank.

All the managers, personal financial advisors, treasurers, loan officers, and auditors, who were all men that held prestigious positions were already there, including Sebastian, the Tax Accountant IV. The bank wasn't scheduled to open until twenty minutes later. Brandy also strolled in early and noticed Satin at her cage; it was as if Brandy had gotten the early bird memo as well.

"Well hello there, welcome back!" Brandy nudged Satin, shoulder to shoulder. "I have breakfast, want some?" She stopped at her station right next to Satin.

"No thank you, I'm good and I am soooo glad to be back; you have no idea," Satin stressed as she organized her station and filled the deposit/withdrawal slip holders.

"No, I don't, because I don't understand for the life of me, how you are so excited to deal with The General. Nothing has changed since you've been away, you know. If anything, it's gotten worse after the bank robbery and all," Brandy spoke as she gave Satin the typical sassy side eyes and perched lips.

"Unlike most, I can't afford to miss another paycheck like some of us can," Satin teased Brandy as she implied her going out with men for money. "About the robbery though… did they ever catch the guys who did it?" she continued.

Brandy swiftly looked around. She noticed all the office doors were wide open, including Sebastian's. She didn't want anyone to overhear what she had to say. Satin had only been away for a week, but so much had changed around the bank since then.

"Why don't you come with me to the break room so I can catch you up to speed since you've been away?" Brandy walked off, holding her breakfast.

"Okay," Satin responded as she followed Brandy, but she was also confused by her remark. Satin and Brandy entered the break room. Satin took a seat first as Brandy placed her breakfast on the table, then walked over to the coffee machine and fixed her a cup.

"I know you don't usually drink coffee, but I suggest that you may want to get you a cup, because you are not ready for the tea I'm about to spill, hunty," Brandy teased.

"Oh, my, what the heck has been going on around here? I've been missing everything. Why didn't you just call and inform me? You call me 'bout everything else," Satin raised from her seat, walked over to the coffee pot and poured herself a half cup of coffee. "Nah, you know I'm not going to drink this mess, but I guess I'll go along with your theatrics for now," she pestered.

"Bahaha…" Brandy laughed out loud.

"Sshhh! Wasn't the whole purpose of us coming in here was because you didn't want anyone to hear us?" Satin taunted with a whisper as she placed her finger on her lips like a Kindergarten teacher for Brandy to hush.

"Yeah, you're right, but your ass got jokes this morning. Any who… brace yourself bestie, because I really don't think you're ready for this one."

Satin walked back to the table with her cup of coffee and sat. "Okay, okay… I'm listening." She placed the cup in front of her on the table, relaxed and folded her arms across her chest. Brandy sat in a chair next to Satin so she could whisper the office gossip.

"Well, you know the bank was robbed and everything. You also know that I was at lunch, and didn't see anything. I only heard about it once I got back and the place was ambushed with cops. I'm surprised you didn't see it on the news or anything."

"I don't watch too much of television besides *PBS* or *Nick Jr,* thanks to Noah."

"Right, right… but hunty listen to this."

Satin gave Brandy her undivided attention. She usually didn't entertain gossip, but was eager to hear what Brandy had to say. Satin didn't blink or move an eye muscle. Her face was glued to Brandy's face, and the anticipation of big news intrigued her.

Brandy continued, "So, everyone knew that you were suspended, and everyone knew that Sebastian was somewhere other than work, because no one really knew what was going on with him after that wedding."

"Right," Satin agreed.

"Well, the next day after the robbery, everyone who was present at the bank was questioned. I was even questioned; although I was not inside of the bank at the time, but The General gave the police a list of everyone who was scheduled to be at work that day, also the ones who were not scheduled. I guess, they called themselves covering all the basics."

"Right," Satin agreed again.

"Any who… here's where it gets interesting. Word is that one of the tellers, not sure which one, because no one wants to give a name, but word did get out that one of the tellers recognized the voice of one of the men."

Satin's mouth dropped open. "What! Really?" she questioned with raised eyebrows.

"Shhh… yes, really," Brandy whispered as she shushed her. "Well, no one saw who the men were exactly; but it was two of them

144

and they were wearing all black and face masks. Any who… one did speak, according to the teller. I guess he spoke and said open the drawer and give me the money or some shit like that. At least, that's what I'm guessing."

"Yeah probably so," Satin continued to agree as she became engrossed in Brandy's gossip.

"Girlll… why did the teller say that the voice of the man she heard sounded like the voice of someone who works here at the bank?"

Satin's eyes widened and her mouth fell open again with a gasp. "Get out of here. So… they are trying to say it was an inside job?"

"Yes, pretty much, and that the inside man was Sebastian. Pow, how do you like that spill of tea?"

Satin slid all the way back in the chair as her arms fell at her waist side. She did not speak for at least ten seconds. Satin could not believe what Brandy had just told her. All kind of thoughts ran through Satin's head. She was just starting to like Sebastian and couldn't believe that the man she helped and started a friendship with was even capable of something like robbing the same bank that he worked at.

In Satin's eyes, Sebastian didn't fit the bill, but she knew no one knew everything about anyone. Looks were deceiving and so were personalities. Satin knew she wasn't the best judge of character, but Sebastian had great characteristics and appeared to be a standup kind of guy. Hearsay around the bank caused some to question his authenticity and may have even planted some doubt in Satin.

"Well... I see cat got your tongue," Brandy teased.

Satin scooted her chair back to the table. "Um... I am definitely surprised to hear that. I mean... really... are they even sure? How could they even be so sure of something like that? That's a pretty serious accusation to be throwing around like that without any kind of sound proof" Satin justified and didn't hesitate to express her concerns.

"Right, it is. Fittingly, you know how Sebastian, Mr. Frank, Mr. Alex, and Mr. Paul, that whole little upscale clique would normally lunch together and everything, right?"

"Yeah, before I left, before I..." Satin caught herself before she said too much about the friendship her and Sebastian began to start.

"Before you what?"

"Uhhh... nothing. I'm just really stunned about something like this. I mean... the guy is going through a very difficult time in his life. *We* all know that around here even though some of us could care less about anyone else other than themselves. Why would anyone just assume it was him just because the robbery took place while he was obviously taking time off after dealing with something in his personal life? Those bank robbers could have been anyone.

Anyone of their behinds who work here, if you ask me. Putting the blame on Sebastian appears to be a call of convenience, you think?"

"Well, it's obvious who side you are on," Brandy responded defensively. She couldn't understand why Satin was so defensive about Sebastian all of a sudden and had become his protector just because she spent some time with him at his home.

Satin looked at Brandy oddly. "You say that as if the man is already trialed and juried. I'm just stating the obvious. Sebastian… no, Mr. Smith, since you referred to everyone else he hangs out with by their last name, doesn't cross me as that kind of person. Anddd… besides the fact that he makes pretty good damn money as an accountant already. That's crazy. Why would he feel the need to rob the same bank where he works? Just doesn't make any sense if you ask me."

"You did say, it could have been anyone. He is anyone, he, as in Mr. Smith, that is," Brandy sassed.

Satin began to irritate Brandy, and she was about done with the conversation since Satin's mind was already made up about something she knew nothing about because she was not there when it happened.

Satin ignored Brandy's sarcasm. "So, you think the man is guilty too?"

"I'm just saying. I wasn't here, and no I didn't see anything or hear anyone's voice. I'm just going by what everyone else is saying. The ones who *were* here doing the robbery."

"Well you know what they say."

"No, I don't and who is they and what do they say?" Brandy asked as she kept her defense armor on tight with no intentions of adjusting it.

"Well… *they* say that *we* all look alike and sound alike. So yeah, it could have been anyone." Satin answered as she, too, kept her defense armor of shielding her new friend, Sebastian, on tightly.

Ohhh… white people, Brandy thought to herself. "Listen bestie, I'm not completely convinced that it was ole boy, okay? However, I'm not ruling him out either. And your all of a sudden sense to protect him is rather interesting, I must say."

Satin gave Brandy a bizarre stare and Brandy challenged the look down without a blink of an eye. Satin didn't have anything else to say about the topic as she struggled within to process all what Brandy had just informed her of.

Someone walked through the door of the break room and interrupted the two tellers stare down.

"Speaking of the devil," Brandy whispered underneath her breath, but Satin heard every word.

"Good morning, ladies," Sebastian spoke in a relaxed tone as he stood by the table, well dressed in his tailored business suit.

Sebastian's clean-cut fade enhanced his already handsome face, and the lining of his beard put the final touches on a well sculpted piece of body art. Sebastian was the attractive combination of vitality and sexy. He looked as if he had just walked off the cover of GQ magazine and smelled like every woman's fantasy.

"Good morning," Brandy and Satin spoke simultaneously.

Satin took in Sebastian's handsomeness as Brandy watched her melt like butter on the outside. The eyes didn't lie and it was very evident that Satin found Sebastian mouth-wateringly delicious. Sebastian had a stimulating glow about himself and it caught the lady's attention.

"Welcome back, Satin. It's good to see you back at work."

"Thank you, I'm glad to be back," Satin quickly responded.

Brandy observed the obvious temptation that was infusing between Satin and Sebastian right before her very own eyes. They gawked at each other as if they wanted to consume one another right on top of the break room table. Satin tried her damnedest to hide the attraction to her co-worker, but Brandy wasn't buying it at all, especially since she witnessed how Sebastian looked at Satin.

"Looks like I just walked up on something. I'll just get my coffee and the two of you can get back to whatever it was you were discussing before I walked in," Sebastian teased.

"Don't leave on our account. We weren't discussing much, you know... nothing but shopping, typical girl stuff," Brandy fibbed and smiled as she checked Sebastian out from head to toe herself. *Uh uh uhn... just all kinds of yummy.*

Satin nudged Brandy's leg underneath the table when she realized Sebastian knew exactly what she was doing. Brandy flinched. Satin kept her mouth closed and continued to watch Sebastian as she slowly exhaled. The accountant was simply irresistible and had the smarts and bank account to match it.

"Right. Well, I hope you ladies have a wonderful day," Sebastian uttered as he solely zoomed in on Satin.

"You do the same," Brandy responded. She noticed Satin just staring back at Sebastian. Brandy hit her on the leg underneath the table to knock her out of daze.

"Uh yeah, sure, I hope you have a wonderful day as well," Satin finally responded as she came out of her daydream. Sebastian smiled and walked over to the coffee pot. He poured a cup, left it black with no sugar and walked back to his office.

Damn... just like I like my man, tall, dark and hot. "What the hell was that! Are you still going to lie to me and tell me *nothing* happened at Sebastian's when you *supposedly* were only there to check up on him? If your eyes were a BB gun, you would have shot the man's eyes right out," Brandy jested.

Satin slowly raised from her chair. She picked up the cup of coffee she never drank, poured it out in the sink and disposed the paper container. "You are soooo dramatic, you know that? I told you, *nothing happened.*"

"That didn't look like *nothing* to me."

Brandy rose from the table and disposed her empty cup and placed the food in the refrigerator that she never got a chance to eat because she was gossiping.

"I guess your breakfast has become lunch, eh?" Satin changed the subject.

"I guess it has, but we will continue this conversation at lunch time."

"No, we will not, nosey Rosy. Let me just say this in case you forgot. I have a man, and Sebastian just went through a great loss in his life. He can't possibly be thinking about a new woman at this time, or anytime soon, for that matter. He's probably getting back with his ex anyway. Who knows?"

"Girl, that woman left that man at the altar. That *fine ass* man, that is. They not getting back together, trust me."

"And you knowww this becauseee…"

"I just know these types of things, darling. I know if I were him, I wouldn't take someone back who left me at the altar."

"Well, whether they are getting back together or not, which is none of my business, I have a man and I'm not looking for a new one," Satin covered her contempt for Nolan with a lie.

She had begun to despise Nolan, and was deeply hurt by what he had done to her, but her personal life at home was none of Brandy's business.

"All in all, he's a bachelor as of recently, and I'm sure a man like that won't be available much longer. Look at him, too damn fine and he smelled so good." *I wonder what he was wearing?*

"Well, according to you, based on what *everybody else* thinks around here, he's a sure criminal. Now, what would any woman in her right mind want with a criminal?"

"Girlllll, those be the best ones. Girl, that thug loving gives me the business, believe that. You should know; you got one now."

"Girl, bye," Satin uttered and walked out of the break room.

Janice left her personal office and made her way towards Satin. Satin stopped in the middle of the path back to her cage, with hopes of addressing the boss. Satin's intentions were in the right place. She had high hopes of clearing the air of bad vibes that was caused before the suspension.

"Good morning, Janice. I'm so glad…"

Before Satin could finish her sentence, Janice strode right past and didn't have the decency to say one word, as if she was hard of hearing. She ignored Satin and kept her face looking straight forward without a turn in any direction. Janice never felt an ounce of un-sportsmanship toward the girl who worked underneath her; she'd already made her mind up about Satin, and had no plans of changing her perception of her.

"Ooookay… that went well," Satin said out loud as a trivial smile graced her face.

She was determined not to let anything or anyone ruin her day and that included Janice. On Satin's way to her station, with only ten minutes left before the bank opened, she walked past Sebastian's office. Something in her spirit spoke to her and she immediately turned around.

Satin stepped in front of Sebastian's opened door.

"KNOCK KNOCK," Satin spoke as she stood in front of the door.

Sebastian slid his leather chair closer to his desk and greeted Satin with his eyes. He was a bit surprised that she came to his office door after not saying much in the break room.

"Hey, come on in," Sebastian offered up an open invitation with enthusiasm. "What can I do for you Miss Satin, or is it Mrs. Satin since we never got to that question at dinner?"

"Just Satin is fine, and no Sir, I'm not a Mrs."

"Well, that doesn't explain why you ignored my text this weekend. Step into the office and close the door if you don't mind, please?" Sebastian politely asked. He was left with a lot of unanswered questions and wanted to address them.

Satin stepped all the way into the office, but did not close the door as Sebastian suggested. "I won't be long, and I'm sorry if I disturbed you."

"No, you're good. I'm just getting ready for a morning meeting. How about you, are you okay? You know… I hate to admit this, but um… I was actually a bit worried about you after not hearing from you. I didn't know if you made it back home safe or not. I didn't know if you were in trouble with your man or not. I mean... I thought we had fun that day getting to know one another."

"Yeah, about that. Listen, Sebastian... I'm sorry I didn't return any of your texts, and to be perfectly honest, I feel really guilty about that. As you said, we did have fun together, but it's just... my life is complicated right now and obviously, yours is, too.

"Satin, please close the door and have a seat if you will?"

"You're not worried about what everyone around here would think of us two closed up in your office together?"

"Baby girl, listen... Do I look like I'm a man who is concerned with what everybody thinks? The only person I'm concerned with what she thinks at this moment is standing in front of me. Now go on and close that door. I have a meeting in five minutes to get to. I promise, this won't take long."

Satin gazed through the glass windows of Sebastian's office. She noticed Brandy eyeing the two of them and a couple of other women tellers who were shoo shooing while looking their way. Satin shook her head at Brandy, and walked to the door and closed it. She stood in front of Sebastian's desk.

"Is it okay that I continue to stand?"

"If you're comfortable with that, sure."

"I am," Satin smiled.

"Well in that case, I will stand, too," Sebastian said as he rose from the comfort of his leather chair and stood from behind the desk.

He confidently walked around to the front of desk. Satin backed up. She got nervous, and unlike Sebastian, she did care what everyone else thought of the two of them locked inside of his office together. The shades were opened and the window and door was glass.

"Would you like me to close the blinds?" Sebastian pestered.

"No, no, please don't, Sebastian."

Sebastian chuckled as he leaned on his desk and crossed his legs and relaxed his hands on the edge of the wooden desk. "Come here."

Satin looked at Sebastian oddly. "You want... ah... you want me to come closer to you?" Satin stumbled on her words.

"Yes, I do, Satin. Don't worry, I won't kiss you or anything like that. I just want you to come closer so I can look you in your eyes and say what I need to say."

"Okayyy..." Satin said as she slowly stepped closer towards Sebastian.

Sebastian uncrossed his legs, leaned off the desk, and stood in front of Satin. He pierced her pure eyes with his. Sebastian took in all Satin's loveliness just as she took in his handsomeness.

"You're so beautiful, you know that? I don't know why I didn't notice you in this way before. I probably would have saved myself from the heartbreak I'm enduring now." Satin was surprised at the heavy compliment that Sebastian laid on her and became bashful. She closed her eyes as her jawbone hit her chest.

"Chin up, baby girl. You have nothing to be embarrassed about. You are beautiful and any sane man can see that, even the wounded and broken hearted have eyes."

Satin raised her head and slightly smiled at Sebastian. She loved everything he said to her. Sebastian was gentle, street, smart, classy and one of the most successful men in the building. Satin had begun to fall and didn't even know it.

"Um… you said you had something you wanted to say to me?" she asked, trying to downplay her interest in Sebastian.

"Yeah, I just did. Well, that was part of it. I really don't want to be late for this meeting, so we must continue this conversation at lunch. Will you have lunch with me?"

"Lunch? Uhhh… I don't know…"

"Come on, it's just lunch. You know, like it was just dinner. I promise I won't bite, although I am very tempted."

Oh, my goodness, could you not be any more appealing. "Sebastian…"

"I'm not taking no for an answer, my beautiful Satin. Have lunch with me? I know you only get thirty minutes to my hour, so that will give me enough time to order the food and have it waiting for you at the restaurant."

"But you don't know what kinds of food I like?"

"You'd be surprise the things I pick up on within a minute of knowing someone. Other than the fact that a woman I was in love with was still in love with her ex, but that don't count," Sebastian teased.

"It's cute how you can joke about this now," Satin tittered.

"Oh, believe me. I joke about it to keep from crying. Now, have lunch with me, woman?"

"Okay, okay… I'll have lunch with you, Sebastian."

"Great. I'll text you the address. It's only a couple of blocks away from here. It will take you less than two minutes. You probably would enjoy the walk, if you're a walker."

"I'm not, I'll drive." *Although I do enjoy walking at the park.*

"Well, suit yourself. I'll see you at lunch," Sebastian said as he walked to the door and opened it for Satin. She made it to the door.

"I would kiss you on your cheek, but I won't since you're all worried about what everyone thinks around here."

Satin smiled and kissed Sebastian on his cheek instead. *Oh, my God! Did I just do that?* Satin internally chastised herself as Sebastian slightly smiled.

Satin walked out Sebastian's office and dreaded the fact that she had to explain herself to nosey Brandy, who was waiting for her to return to the station.

Chapter Fourteen

Keep Your Friends Close and Enemies Closer

Frank had called an emergency meeting to discuss the financial crisis that Bank of America was facing due to lawsuits and investigations regarding mortgages, financial disclosures and the recent robbery. The bank chain owed $16.65 billion in lawsuits and damages, and was considering making some employees cuts. The recent robbery didn't help, and Frank wanted to let the staff know the financial deficit that they were facing. Lay-offs were in the works and bonuses were on hold until further notice.

Sebastian was running a few minutes behind schedule after Satin surprised him with a visit to his office. He knew he had a meeting to get to, but was curious as to why she didn't return any of his texts. Sebastian would normally be one of the first at the table waiting on the others, but that day, he was distracted by Satin and needed to see her before attending the weekly meeting.

He walked in the conference room prepared, confident and looking like a bag of money. Sebastian seemed as though he didn't have a worry in the world, although he believed the front runners were running a conspiracy theory against him. Sebastian convinced himself that he was there for one reason and one reason only; to do his job as the bank's tax accountant, so their perception of him was none of his concern. His spreadsheets were on point and he was over prepared to give his input once it was his time to speak.

One thing Sebastian knew for certain, he never failed at doing his job and wasn't bothered that Frank, Paul, nor Alex undermined him every chance they got. They were all sitting around the table, including Janice and a few others, as if they were all plotting against him, but was really just having small talk that particular morning. The tension was air thick and egos were at an all-time high.

Sebastian graced them with his commanding presence and Frank cleared his throat as if it was a sign for him to start the meeting. Frank had haunted squinted eyes, loose fold ruddy facial skin as if it was sunburned and often associated with old age. He definitely looked like an elderly man, but was only in his early fifties. Frank waited for Sebastian to take his seat and then he stood before the board.

"Good morning gentleman… and ladies," Frank spoke with a firm tone as he looked around the room and acknowledged everyone.

He continued. "I would like to just say, due to the recent unfortunate incident, I want to thank everyone for doing a fantastic job with staying calm, being diligent and continuing to make sure that the customers always come first, regardless as to what may be going on behind the scenes here at BOA. I also want to take this time and address the big elephant in the room. As of last week, as most of you already know, there is an ongoing investigating regarding the robbery, and I've been working persistently with the police department to provide as much information as I can to make sure the people or persons who are responsible for such hideous crime be brought to justice," he paused. "And let me just throw this out there, so there won't be any more misunderstandings. I know there's a lot of talk around here about what happened or what did not happen, but just know that we are not accusing any one, and it is proper protocol to question every employee. Needless to say, *everyone* is under investigation at this point and no one is excluded; including me," Frank spoke, but was lying about him being under investigation. He only wanted to put the rumors to bed and didn't want anyone to feel as though they were a sure person of interest.

Frank went on to talk about the financial problems the bank was facing and how they were going to implement some necessary changes including laying a few people off, but mainly employees whose jobs were not as significant as of those who were in the meeting.

Sebastian listened, but didn't completely buy the part where Frank said he himself was under investigation. Sebastian glanced over at Alex and Paul and noticed they seemed to be in agreement with what Frank had to say because he caught a sneaky grin Paul gave to Frank when he looked over at him.

Sebastian realized that was the second time the conversation was being had, and the first time was only between Frank, Alex, and Paul; alone. Sebastian was convinced that they had concocted a way to try and make him feel as though he wasn't the only one being investigated, although he knew better. Sebastian went along with the meeting, and acted as though he hadn't caught a white lie.

After forty-five minutes, Frank concluded the meeting and everyone raised from their chair, everyone but Sebastian. He remained seated and answered a text message he received from Satin that made him smile. She told him she knew how boring meetings were and wanted to be his distraction with a lot of funny face emojis. Sebastian told her she was a good distraction to have and was looking forward to lunch.

The room cleared, except for Frank and Paul. Sebastian finally raised from his seat and headed towards the door. He noticed that everyone else had gone back to work, except for Frank and Paul. Sebastian walked past them, but Frank called out his name just before he walked out the door.

Sebastian turned around and gave them a look of distrust.

"We're taking an early lunch today; lunch on me. Will you be joining us?" Frank asked with a grimy smirk on his face.

"Naw, I'm good and besides, I've already made plans," Sebastian retorted without hesitation as he and Frank stared each other down. Sebastian didn't offer a smile nor did he give any kind of indication that he would have lunch with them again or any time soon.

Paul just sat back quietly in the black leather chair as he twiddled his pen in between his fingers.

"Okay, but if you change your mind, we'll be at our usual restaurant," Frank answered.

Sebastian just looked.

Keep your friends close and your enemies closer.

"I'll keep that in mind," he responded, and then walked off and returned to his office.

"What was that all about? Do you think he bought it?" Frank asked Paul.

"Maybe, maybe not," he answered.

Frank took his cell out and dialed a number.

"It's done," he spoke in a grave tone and then ended the call.

After, he and Paul raised from the table and went out to lunch with Alex.

Chapter Fifteen

A New Chapter, A New Beginnings

Sebastian soaked in the pleasant weather on the patio at Vintner Grill, a Bar and Bistro. He shot a text to Satin, and provided a list of the lunch menu. She teased him about what he said about knowing what she wanted to eat. Sebastian made fun that the food was way too expensive to mess up, and that she probably would end up re-ordering, and he didn't want to take any chances. Satin sent laughing emojis and chose something off the menu.

Sebastian placed their orders and made sure the waiter didn't bring Satin's food out until she arrived, so it would be fresh and hot. The waiter agreed and did what was asked.

To pass time, Sebastian answered a few emails from his iPhone. He snacked on a house salad and drank lemon water as he waited for Satin's arrival.

Sebastian's thoughts drifted and he begun to think about his encounter with Satin in his office. He convinced himself that he had to be careful with Satin because he was not in a position emotionally to pursue anything with any woman; his heart was still with Angela. Sebastian swayed himself to believe he was just enjoying Satin's friendship, and wouldn't try anything with her that would cross the lines of only being friends. Satin had already kissed him on the cheek by then, and the thin line of just friends was slowly disappearing.

Sebastian's phone rung and he was surprised to see the number that appeared on his touchscreen. With hesitation, he swiped the green arrow to answer.

"Hello?" he responded in an assertive strong tone.

"Hi, Sebastian."

"What is it, Angela? Why are you calling me?" Sebastian questioned with a harsh tone.

"I umm… I was calling to make sure you were okay. I've been worried about you, Sebastian, and the way we left things. I don't know… I guess I kind of feel like we didn't have proper closure."

"Closure! Proper closure? Leaving me at the damn altar gave me all the closure I need, Angela. Listen, and I'm only going to say this once… I'm no longer your concern, Angie. Don't call me ever again. This bullshit is for the birds, man!" Sebastian thundered as he hung up the phone in Angela's face.

The fucking audacity of that woman. What the fuck could we possibly have to talk about now? Sebastian thought to himself as he sat back in his chair and thought about all the things he told himself he would say to Angela if he'd ever spoken to her again, but once the opportunity presented itself, Sebastian had nothing at all to say to the woman who broke his heart.

He loosened his tie and tried to calm his anger that was brewing inside of him.

The phone rang again and it was Angela calling back.

"What we not gon' do is play this stupid ass game." Sebastian rejected Angela's call and placed her number on the block list. *Why you trying me, you already know I aint that nigga; kick rocks.*

When Sebastian was loving Angela, he was loving her and only her. By then, Sebastian was full of anger towards Angela, and his pride would not get out of the way. She had hurt him beyond measures, and betrayed the trust that Sebastian believed they had together. Sebastian never thought in a million years he would have a heart of stone towards Angela, the woman he once thought the world of. But just then, he found himself trading the lines of resentment towards Angela, and there was no turning back the hands of time.

Sebastian was going through the motions, and was trying his damndest to handle the situation like a man, and not overreact, which would have caused him to get locked up.

Satin walked in and her eyes scanned the beautiful restaurant. She texted Sebastian to let him know she had arrived. Sebastian answered that he was out on the patio, waiting.

Satin walked to the patio. Sebastian got up, and pulled the chair out for her to sit. She took a seat and noticed the waiter walking towards them. The waiter took Sebastian's instructions seriously, and was watching their table like an eagle; he reacted as soon as he noticed a woman had taken her seat at the table. The waiter placed their foods in front of them, and Satin was pleased, and felt as though Sebastian was taking care of her every want and need. Sebastian had eaten his salad, but had little room left in his belly for more.

"Ohhh... this all looks so tasty," Satin smiled.

"This is one of my favorite spots to grab lunch or dinner; dig in."

Satin and Sebastian enjoyed their lunch and was full as a tick. Satin glanced around the restaurant and noticed how nice the place was.

"I have never been here before. I didn't even realize this place was here while driving to work," Satin spoke as she reached for the glass of Raspberry Tea and took a sip.

"Man, this place is the shit. I eat here all the time. I thought we could enjoy a little fresh air. You know, we only get this kind of weather during this time of year. These deserts are usually hot as hell."

"Right, it's really nice out here and the weather is beautiful. Umm... to switch gears for a minute, I noticed before today, that is, that you always go to lunch with guys from the bank who do what you do, and dress like you dress."

Sebastian slightly chuckled. "Speak on it, baby girl, don't beat around the bush. What exactly are you saying, Miss Satin?" Satin chuckled as well. She knew Sebastian picked up on her subliminal hit towards him and wanted her to be specific.

"I'm just saying... before I had gotten to know you in all, I realized that you don't socialize much, other than the people who sit in offices like you do and dress like you dress. I guess what I'm really saying is... I thought you were full of yourself, and your circle of friends were too," Satin faulted, not holding back on her previous impression of Sebastian.

"Aw baby girl, you think you know, but you have no idea, do you? Looks can really be deceiving most times. You know, the same people you speak of, the people you say are my friends? Well, those same people are investigating me right now, do you know that?"

"The robbery?"

"Yes, the robbery."

"Yes, I know about that," Satin answered. "So, your friends are investigating you?"

"Friends? Don't get it twisted, love. Just because you are on the outside looking in, don't assume you know what's really going on behind the scenes."

"Oh?"

"Yes, I say what I mean and mean what I say. So, you see me leaving with a group of guys I work with, having lunch together, and you just quick to assume that we are friends? Negative, those same men question EVERYTHING I do. They judge me, just as they judge every other young black man from the street. I guess we all are thugs, no matter how many degrees we may obtain, or how many obstacles we cross and prove ourselves; to them, we're all thugs."

Satin's eyes broadened.

"You're surprised? How could you be? Wake up, baby girl, you're asleep. It doesn't matter how much a young black man has been through, or how many degrees he may obtain, as I've said, the white older man at the top will still, and always, question our motives and possibilities. No matter how many times I show these people I earn every dollar I make, every cent in my bank account, to them, I'm still just another young, black male from the street, the hood, rather. And to be more specific, do you know, all the money I have made for that bank, all the reports that they questioned, but did not find *any* discrepancies ever, they now somehow assume that I was one of the guys who robbed the place. Are you fucking kidding me? Yeah, I'm the accountant from Bank of America. The youngest, who just so happens to be black, and they all look at me as if I'm some kind of motherfucking criminal? Where is the fucking justice?" Sebastian spoke with passion.

Satin just sat and stared. She thought Sebastian had a better position than her without realizing what was really going on behind the scenes. She didn't know what to say and didn't want to say the wrong thing. She just gazed.

"I'm sorry, I don't mean to get all crazy about this. I do tend to get passionate when I'm pissed, and especially about this new bullshit of speculation they seem to amuse themselves with at my expense. I know you didn't know all of this, but it just trips me out how we as people think we know, but don't have no idea about something going on right underneath our noses."

"Yeah, you're right. I'm sorry, I apologize for assuming and jumping to conclusions without asking first. I just thought... well, one of them I know. Well, not really know per say, but the guy Paul Williams is the husband of a lady who helped me get the job. I just figured he was a good guy."

"Nah, you're good. I don't blame you, but it's only because you're so damn cute," Sebastian joked to lightened the intensity that he caused. "Paul... Paul is the worst of them all. His ass is a house nigga if I ever saw one. You would think he would be on my side, considering the fact that we're both black and can relate to working with white men with power who don't respect the fact that not all black men are thugs we are just as smart and educated as most of them. Believe it or not, Paul gets right with them and agrees with everything they say or do so they'll stay off his ass kissing Uncle Tom black ass. He couldn't beat 'em, so he joined them."

"Oh…wow. I had no idea."

"I know you didn't. Sooo… enough about work and them clowns. Tell me more about you. What happened the other day when you didn't return any of my text?"

Satin gasped. "Uhhhh… can we please talk about something else other than that?"

"I don't think that's fair, Satin. I mean… you damn near know everything about me, and I clearly know nothing about you. You even saw me in my birthday suit *before* we became friends. Hell, you have seen me at my absolute worst, not too many women can ever say that; as a matter of fact, not any. You are already ahead of the game. What you got to lose?" Sebastian teased and Satin slightly smiled. "Listen baby girl, you know I really think you're pretty cool and everything. I would really like to know more about you, but how can I if you won't let me in? Tell me, I really want to get to know you better."

Satin sat in quietness. She knew Sebastian was speaking from a good place and knew she liked him just as he liked her. Before the day, she went over to Sebastian's home, Satin never thought she would begin a friendship with the handsome, young accountant who all the woman around the office whispered about. They all knew he wasn't available to any of them because he was engaged to be married, but that didn't stop them from trying.

Satin started to wonder what it would have been like if she never went over to Sebastian's place that day. She wondered would they ever had said more to each other, other than just good morning. Satin didn't know if Sebastian was only being nice to her, because she tried to help him at his worse or whether he genuinely just liked her for her.

"Can I ask you something, first?" Satin questioned.

"Yes, sure. You can always ask me anything you want?"

"Okay. I need you to be honest with me about something."

"I'm always honest. You don't ever have to worry about that, just ask me."

"Do you think we would be sitting here today if I never came over to your home that day?"

"Ummm… honestly, I'm not sure. I mean… I've seen you around the office, but I was a man who was in love and looking forward to starting my life as a husband with a woman I loved. Don't get me wrong, I'm always a man, and I do have eyes, but I wasn't really checking for new friendships in women. With that being said, I did notice that you were a bit different from the girl you hang out with at work, though."

"Brandy?"

"Yes, her. She always flirted with me on the slick. Her and a couple of the others around there, but I never took any of it seriously because I knew who and what I wanted. But you, you never did. I mean, you would speak in all. But, I think that was just common courtesy, so I didn't allow myself to read any more into that. We work at the same bank; people speak to one another. It's called being cordial."

"True."

"Let me ask you a question," Sebastian probed.

"Okay."

"Do you regret that you came over to my place that day? Do you regret that we are now here, sitting in a restaurant having lunch and forming what I think could be a real true friendship?"

"Uhhh no, not at all."

"So, now tell me, Satin. If you don't regret any of those things I've mentioned, why did you ignore my text after we had dinner? I keep asking because I'm just curious to know what happened from the time you left my place Friday night to the time you returned to work this morning."

"Um, it's complicated, Sebastian." Satin gasped. "I um… I have a boyfriend?"

"Well, I figured that much. Look at you, you're gorgeous and you have a great personality to complement your beauty."

Satin blushed. "Well, when I got home that Friday night, my umm… my boyfriend wasn't too thrilled that I had been out."

"I see. Did he know you were with a man? Did he know you were with a co-worker and nothing happened?"

"No, not exactly. It's just that he got really upset with me because he didn't know where I was at."

Sebastian gazed into Satin's eyes and recognized the signs of a fearful woman. A woman who was scared to be transparent, and allow another man to really get to know the person she was. The good, the bad, or the ugly truth.

Nigga controlling like a motherfucker. "I don't know no other way to be but straight forward, so I'm just going to go ahead and shoot straight from the hip. Does your boyfriend put his hands on you?" Sebastian questioned after mentally familiarizing himself on what an emotionally damaged woman looked like. He saw in Satin the same thing he saw in Angela when they first met.

Satin put her head down for a second. Sebastian was asking questions she wasn't ready to answer or share with anyone. She felt as though she could trust Sebastian. He made her feel comfortable and at ease, but she still wasn't ready to admit to anyone what she experienced with Nolan. The thought of it angered her, but also reminded Satin what Nolan was capable of.

Satin slowly raised her head and a tear escaped her eyes. Sebastian noticed Satin's sadness and immediately got up from his seat. He slid his chair right next to Satin and sat in arms reach beside her.

"Baby girl, is that what's happening? Talk to me, did your boyfriend hit you?" Sebastian probed with sincerity.

Sebastian silently hoped that wasn't the case. He didn't want Satin to be one of those women who was stuck in an abusive relationship and didn't know how to leave out of fear. He thought a lot of Satin and wanted better for her.

Satin wiped her tears. She took in a deep breath and let a breath out slowly. "I don't know, not exactly I guess. Ugh... I hate this. I can't believe I'm even talking about this. I haven't shared this with anyone."

Sebastian placed his arm around Satin's chair. He placed his other hand on top of her hand that was resting in her lap. Satin inhaled Sebastian's fine cologne and sincere energy.

"Listen to me, and listen to me carefully. You are better than that if that's what's happening. Don't let no man treat you less than your worth. Don't accept no man putting his hands on you, never," Sebastian spoke, and more tears began to form in Satin's eyes.

Sebastian grabbed Satin by the hand and stood her up.

"You need to get out of that relationship. I don't know all the details, but what I see in front of me is a scared unhappy young woman. Leave his ass, don't let him get away with putting his hands on you. You're so much better than that, baby girl."

Satin was full. She hadn't realized before lunch that she would be crying to Sebastian about what happened to her. She didn't know that she would find an understanding friendship in a man she barely knew. The tears wouldn't stop falling, no matter how much Satin tried to stop them. She was angry at herself because she couldn't stop them and Sebastian had gotten a glimpse into her wounded soul.

Sebastian grabbed Satin and hugged her tight. "It's okay, baby girl. I'm here for you, just as you were there for me. It will be okay; you will get through this. I will help you in any way I can, love," Sebastian promised as he looked Satin deep into her eyes.

"He raped me," a troubled whisper escaped Satin's mouth.

Sebastian's bushy eyebrows raised into his temple. His eyes enlarged and heart sunk. Sebastian allowed Satin's words to marinate and immediately grabbed the leather black check case from the table. He looked at the cost of their meals and reached for his wallet. He left cash for the food, plus a huge tip in the black case.

Sebastian then grabbed Satin by the hand, and escorted her out the restaurant. He walked Satin to her car and they stood in front of it. "Satin, did you report this? Did you call the police?"

Satin responded without thought or no hesitation. "No, he's my son's father and I didn't want to send him to jail. And besides, I wasn't really sure what it was at first."

"Just because he's your son daddy doesn't give dude the right to do that to you. Do you understand that?" *What the hell you mean you're not sure if you were raped or not?*

"Yes, I know. That's why I didn't want to talk about this. I knew what others would say if I told someone. You don't understand the situation. It's just… I've been through so much already, and I'm not sure about how to handle this right now. I don't want my son to lose his dad because of me."

"Damn… this nigga has really done a number on you. Baby girl, reporting a nigga who put his hands on you and raped you is not a good father figure for your son anyway. Wow… your son is probably a lot better off without that kind of influence in his life, daddy or not. Don't settle love, don't settle. You and your son deserve a hell of a lot better than that."

Satin just stared and didn't say anymore. She knew Sebastian was right, but wasn't ready to face the music when it came down to Nolan. She regretted even mentioning what happened, but her conscious was on overload and ready to explode. Sebastian just so happened to be the one it came out to.

"Umm… I think I should go on and get back to work. I really don't want to ruin my probation."

"Damn? You're on probation, too?"

"Yeah, I am."

Sebastian leaned in and hugged Satin again. "I'm here if you need me. I just want you to know that," he spoke and placed a warm friendly peck on Satin's forehead.

Sebastian opened Satin's door and waited for her to take a seat in the car. His passionate eyes leered at her as he secretly wished he could do more. Sebastian closed the door, walked off, and hopped into his Stingray Metallic Corvette that harmonized his grey suit perfectly. He waited for Satin to pull off before he sped off into the mid-day.

Satin strapped herself with the seatbelt as she gazed through the window and caught Sebastian laid back in his seat staring at her.

Damn, you're so sweet, almost too good to be true. I really enjoy spending time with you and now you may look at me differently.

Satin drove back to work. She started to feel ashamed that she opened up to Sebastian. She didn't want Sebastian to view her under that kind of light. Satin felt exposed and couldn't take back anything she disclosed. She felt naked although she was fully dressed.

Satin finished her work day and returned home to take care of Noah. Nolan continued to stay out until all hours of night and expected Satin to be there when he decided to come home. The dynamics of Satin and Nolan's relationship, never changed and he continued to treat Satin the way she allowed him to. There was no true commitment and no respect for her or their relationship.

Chapter Sixteen
When the Shit Hits the Fan

Satin and Sebastian barely said anything to each other after their lunch date. Satin pulled back and Sebastian allowed her the space he felt she needed. They would speak to one another, and Sebastian would ask her was everything okay, just to check up on her. Satin would lie and say, "Yes, everything is good." Sebastian did not read more into what Satin was not saying, he hoped all was well as Satin stated because he hated seeing her cry that day.

Two weeks had passed and Satin was fulling her job responsibilities since she didn't have any more trouble with a baby sitter for Noah. Janice didn't applaud Satin for a job well done, nor did she lighten up on the young mother. Janice figured, before it was over, Satin would soon mess up again, and she already had her pink slip signed and was waiting to date it.

Sebastian received a surprise visit from Angela and he wasn't too happy about it. He asked her to leave and she begged him to just give her a chance as she tried to explain what she was feeling and why she felt the need to not go through with their wedding. Sebastian's wasn't letting up and he told Angela that she was no longer welcomed in his home and not to return. Angela even tried to seduce Sebastian, and he fell for it for a moment, then realized what she was doing and quickly kicked her out.

Sebastian told Angela she was a confused woman who needed extensive counseling, and he didn't have any more time or room in his life for her toxic. Angela was still in love with her abusive ex, and felt the need to be with him, but she knew she had a good man in Sebastian and wished she could somehow have them both.

Angela didn't want another woman to benefit from all that Sebastian had to offer, and tried to pull at his heart strings, but Sebastian wasn't having it. He wanted all or nothing, but concluded that his heart could no longer afford Angela and her problems.

Sebastian had enough worries with what was happening at work, and wasn't willing to co-sign or volunteer for the extra stress with Angela, although his heart was still having trouble letting her go completely. Sebastian chose to ignore what his heart wanted, and instead let his ego guide him into what he believed would get him over Angela, once and for all.

Meanwhile, while Satin was putting in hours at work, Noah forgot his favorite toy at home and was acting out with Karen. She tried everything to calm him down, but Noah wanted his toy. He always fell asleep with it and looked for it when he woke up. Karen called Satin at worked and asked her what did she suggest. Satin told Karen to use the key she left in Noah's bag, and go across the hall to get the toy if she thought it would calm Noah down. Karen agreed and took Noah out to the hall so he wouldn't wake little Darius from his nap as they grabbed the toy.

Noah quieted down as Karen used the key to open the door. Once entered, she heard strange sounds coming from the bedroom. Karen had just spoken to Satin while she was still at work, and from her understanding, Noah's dad was supposed to be at work, too.

The mysterious low voices put Karen in high alarm. She quickly left out of the apartment and put Noah in the playpen with a cookie. It kept him quiet for the time being as Karen went into the hallway closet and grabbed her wooden bat. Karen didn't know why there were sounds coming out of Satin's apartment, but she was damned sure going to find out.

Karen sauntered out her apartment again, and left the door slightly opened so she could hear the kids if they cried. She slowly opened Satin's door again and softly tiptoed in with her bat cocked and ready to hit a home run.

Karen left Satin's front door opened and tread softly towards the bedroom. The room door was slightly opened. She peeped through to see if she saw anyone, and to possibly stop them if they were attempting to rob Satin out of her goodies.

Karen's eyes darted through the slight opening of the door, and noticed a young naked girl straddled on top of Nolan. He was laid back like he was a king in a castle, and enjoying a wild ride.

Karen swiftly pushed the door all the way open as the sound of it releasing startled them both. The girl swiftly slid on the side of Nolan with puzzled eyes and a jaw dropped mouth as she tried to grab the sheet to cover her nakedness. Nolan sat up with furious eyes and looked at Karen like she was crazy.

"What the fuck are you doing old woman, are you lost?" Nolan asked as he mean mugged Karen.

Karen continued to hold her bat in eyesight and had no intentions of backing down whatsoever. She gawked at the girl, eye to eye.

"I'm only going to give you less than one minute to put your clothes on and get the hell out of this woman's house. You should be ashamed of yourself, lil girl!"

The naked girl eased out the bed and grabbed her bra, panties, and dress from the floor and quickly ran to the bathroom. Nolan jumped up and slipped into his pants.

"I don't know who the fuck you are, but you better get your old ass up out of here," he stood and continued to mean mug Karen with blazing eyes.

Karen swung the bat and Nolan's reflex quickly kicked in, causing him to duck.

"The next time I won't miss. I'm the woman who babysits your son, jackass. And you would know that if you took the time out and concerned yourself with what goes on in that baby's life."

Nolan looked at Karen and was stunned that he did not recognize her. He never met Karen officially, but did recall Satin saying the neighbor next door was babysitting Noah. He immediately started to consider the repercussion for his lapse of judgement by bringing another woman into his baby mother's home while she was away at work.

"Listen… this is not what it looks like," Nolan tried to cover his ass before Karen made a call to Satin to tell her what was happening in her apartment.

The girl spoke as she came out of the bathroom. "Nolan, I thought you said you and your baby's mother were done?! You are a liar and a poor excuse for a damn man. I can't believe I even fell for your lying a…" The young woman caught herself before she called Nolan a lying ass. She wanted to respect the older woman who just caught them having sex. "You know what… don't call me EVER again, Loser."

"Didn't I tell you, you had less than a minute to get out of here. Your time is up," Karen pressed.

"I'm going, I'm going!" the girl spoke again as she threw her hands up and rolled her eyes at Nolan. She grabbed her purse and walked out the room and then out the front door.

Nolan stood looking stupid, and didn't have the slightest clue as to how he would explain himself to Satin when she found out he brought another woman into her apartment that she invited him to live in with her.

Nolan had lied to the young girl about him and Satin no longer being together. The girl didn't believe him, so Nolan decided to leave work early when he knew Satin wouldn't be home until five hours later. He took the girl to the apartment to prove his lie, and when she questioned Nolan about Satin's clothes, he told her Satin didn't take all her clothes when she left and would get the rest one day soon. What Nolan didn't know was that Satin had left Karen a spare key just in case she forgot something for Noah. Perfect example forgetting to pack Noah's favorite toy in his diaper bag.

"Listen... Mrs. Karen, that's your name, right?"

"Young man, I don't have anything more to say to you. But I will tell you this... You better confess your sins to God first, then to Satin or else I will. And don't go calling disturbing her on that job either. You WAIT until she gets home with all this old foolishness; carrying on around here like you aint got no good sense at all or the ones the good Lord gave to you. WHO RAISED YOU? You tell Satin everything, and I do mean everything or I will," Karen threatened as she lowered her raised arm with the wooden bat and walked out the room.

Karen noticed Noah's favorite toy on the living room couch and grabbed it. She walked out the apartment and went inside her apartment and shut the door. Karen handed Noah his toy and he was excited, but he was unaware that his babysitter had almost knocked his daddy over the head with her bat.

*****

Later that evening, Satin returned home from work, but had to make a stop at the grocery story to pick up dinner. She called Karen to see if she needed anything from the store. Karen told Satin, she was okay on groceries but could use a dozen eggs for a homemade cake she was about to bake for Noah and little Darrius. Karen never mentioned what happened at her apartment during lunch time, and still meant every word she had spoken to Nolan.

Satin made it to the grocery store, picked up her and Noah's dinner, along with the eggs Karen asked for and then drove straight home. She stopped at Karen's as she would normally do in the evenings. Noah was asleep in the playpen while little Darrius watched television in the kitchen with his granny.

"Hey baby, how was your day?" Karen asked, standing at the counter while waiting to mix her batter up for the cake.

Karen didn't know if Satin had already spoken to Nolan or not. She stood and observed Satin's body language to see if she appeared to be irritated. Karen thought about how hard it would be on Satin to have to pay all her bills all on her own. Karen's heart really sympathized with Satin, and she wished there was more she could do to save Satin from the heartache she was about to be stricken with.

Karen believed Satin deserved to know the truth about Nolan, and if after finding out the truth didn't change anything between the two of them, she told herself she had to respect Satin's choices about her life, and not to overstep any boundaries by bad mouthing the father of her child.

Karen had experienced a few fools in her young adult life before she became a saved woman and began to wait for the man she believed God made just for her, who was the father of both of her children.

Karen had also had a baby that died of crib death with a young man before she was married to her deceased husband. The guy dragged Karen through hell and back and Satin reminded her of the woman she was back then. Karen related to Satin in more ways than one, and that's why she had a great deal of empathy towards her.

Karen understood what it was to be twenty years old, and trying to figure out a harsh world as a young mother. Her heart grieved for the Satin, but she prayed to God before Satin arrived that she would not get upset with her for meddling into her personal affairs. Karen even wished that she could take back what happened, but it was already too late, and she owed it to Satin to give her the opportunity to know the truth about a man she claimed she loved.

Satin hadn't spoken to Nolan then and had no clue as to what was in store for her. Satin was glad that a hard day at work was over and she could spend some time with Noah. That was all Satin was looking forward to doing that evening.

"Another day, another dollar, Mrs. Karen," Satin answered. "I can't really complain, other than the fact my boss will not let up on me, but it's okay, I guess she's only doing her job. I just thank God, and I'm so grateful to you that I still have a job."

"I know that's right, sweetheart. What an awesome God we serve," Karen answered as she added the eggs to the cake mixture.

"Amen…amen." Satin agreed in a good mood after not letting anything get to her at work. Satin was filled with positive energy, and was looking forward to what was to come of it. "I see Noah is asleep, huh? I'm sorry, I forgot his toy this morning. I betcha it was that *Incredible Hulk* one, that his favorite of them all."

"Yup, that little green monster he loves more than anything," Karen joked.

Satin tittered as she agreed. "I've been so focused on not being late by going to work early, it slipped my mind to grab it from the sofa. I hope he didn't give you too much trouble."

"Oh, no worry, I could handle a crying toddler who just want a toy that's dear to him. Once Noah got it, he was fine and fell right on to sleep. He woke up forty-five minutes later. I fed him, and he and Darrius played together until Darrius fell asleep on him," Karen chuckled.

Satin grinned, "I know you wish they would both nap at the same time, that would surely be a blessing. I don't see how you do it. Noah weighs me down by himself, I can't even think about what it's like with another one his age. Goodness," Satin joked.

"Oh, I'm quite used to it. I should be by now after raising two of my own and babysitting a bunch of other little snotty noses for years," Karen teased.

"I don't know Mrs. Karen; I wonder whether I will ever get used to being a mother. This is not an easy gig. I wish I would have known before I volunteered," Satin sighed as her lips shuttered.

"No, it's not dear, but you will get used to it. You are doing fine, sugah. You are doing exactly what's expected of you at that age, and considering the situation, it could be a lot worse. Speaking of... I believe the father of your son wants to speak to you. Go on home, no need to wake Noah, I'll just call you when he wakes. You know how Noah gets when he's awakened out of his sleep."

Satin looked at Karen strangely. She was confused as to why Karen would know that Nolan wanted to speak to her at that moment. Nolan texted Satin while she was at work and told her, he wanted to talk to her about something, but it could wait until she got home.

"Yeah, Noah does get snappy, doesn't he? You wake him out of his sleep and he's mad with the world. That's the part of him that he gets from his daddy. Mrs. Karen, did something happen? Did Nolan come over after work to try and pick up Noah or something?"

Karen lightly chortled. "Oh no, nothing like that, sweetheart. I'll just let you have a talk with him and I'm sure Nolan will tell you all about it. Go on now, the cake will be done in twenty minutes. You and your family are welcomed to have some."

"Um…okay," Satin answered as she continued to stare at Karen, confused. She grabbed her purse. "I'll be back, or if Noah wakes before I return, just call me and I'll come and get him."

"Sure thing, I'll definitely do that."

Satin teased little Darrius for a moment and then walked out of Karen's apartment. When Satin walked inside, she noticed Nolan sitting on the couch looking like his dog had just died and was confused as to how he would go on without him.

"Hey, what's up?" Satin spoke as she walked to the kitchen and started to pull out cooking pans to cook dinner.

Nolan sat quietly. He didn't even answer Satin with a spoken word; he didn't know how or if Karen had already informed Satin as she promised. Satin rambled on and on about how her day went at work. She remembered Nolan's text and Karen informing her that he had something to tell her, but Satin was so thrilled that Nolan was home early and would possible eat dinner with her and Noah that she didn't mention what Karen told her or the text she received.

Satin realized Nolan was awfully quiet, and was not in a hurry to leave out as usual. She was rather surprised that he was home at that time of evening, just chilling. She finished washing her chicken breasts, seasoned them and then placed in the oven. Satin walked back to the living room and noticed that Nolan was still sitting in quietness without the television or anything else distracting him.

Satin stood in front of him. "Your awfully quiet, and I gotta say, I'm rather surprised that your even here. Are you staying long enough to eat dinner with me and our son?"

Nolan stared up at Satin. He was looking for the right words to comfort her with his lies and betrayal. "Sit down, Satin," he spoke and patted the spot next to him.

Satin took a seat and looked at Nolan. "Okay, I'm sitting."

"Umm... I don't know how much you know already, but um... I just want you to know that I am very sorry 'bout what happened and nothing like that will ever happen again," Nolan promised.

"Nolan, what are you talking about? You're sorry about what?" Satin questioned as she placed her hands on her thighs.

"She didn't tell you?" Nolan quizzed with widened eyes and raised eyebrows.

"She? Who? Tell me what?"

"The old lady across the hall. She didn't tell you what happened?"

Satin thought again about Karen telling her Nolan needed to talk to her and figured that was what he must have been talking about. Satin knew that Karen always offered up a good word and a helping hand to anyone whom she felt was in need. She started to think that maybe Karen offered Nolan a few words of wisdom as she done with all who appeared to be in distraught.

"Uh no, Mrs. Karen didn't tell me anything. The only thing she told me was that you needed to talk to me about something. What… did you try to go and pick up our son and she offered you some advice or something? She means well Nolan, she really does."

"Is that what she said?" Nolan asked, trying to figure out how he could put a spin to what happened.

"No, Nolan. I told you Mrs. Karen didn't tell me anything other than what I told you. She said you had something to tell me. What is it, because between the both of you not saying whatever it is that needs to be said, I'm starting to get worried. What's the big deal and what's going on, Nolan?"

"Listen baby…"

Satin stared at Nolan with staggered eyes. She was quite astonished that he referred to her as a sweet term of endearment. Her mind realized that something serious must have happened and Nolan was trying to soften the blow. Satin felt as though she needed to brace herself for the unexpected. She continued to stare at Nolan, motionless.

Before that evening, Satin never saw Nolan looking as desperate as he did sitting on the couch. He was at a loss for words and searched deep within for some kind of help to form a sentence. Nolan chose his words carefully; he studied Satin's body language. Satin allowed herself to feel a sense of remorse, but didn't know what it was that Nolan had to say.

"I'm listening, Nolan."

"Baby, I um… I got off a little early today, and I um…"

"You what?" Satin interrupted. *What is the big deal of you leaving work? Get to it already.*

"Well, let me just put this out there. I fucked up, I fucked up big time, and I know for sure now what matters to me the most. That's you and our son. I love you, Satin."

Satin's eyes widened even more. She dreamed of what that moment would be like when, or if, Nolan would ever tell her those three words. Ever since Satin found out she was pregnant with Noah, she yearned to hear Nolan say that to her. Satin wanted to know and believe that she and Noah were the only thing that mattered to Nolan in his life.

Satin didn't know what Nolan was keeping from her, and she was beginning to think that no matter what it was, she would forgive him, and they would work through it together. Satin was ready to move forward and was hell bent on the two of them raising their son together.

Satin had already begun to prepare dinner, and was pleased that Nolan was there confessing his love for her finally. She took deep breaths and let Nolan's words immerse into her mind and heart for a moment.

Satin realized that she could finally put her worries to rest of Nolan leaving her and Noah, because deep down inside, she believed he never wanted to be there to begin with. Satin never denied the fact that Nolan was only their out of convenience. She placed her hand on top of Nolan's.

"Whatever it is, it's okay. We will work past it." Satin had forgiven Nolan for his cheating ways and also for assaulting her. She figured that was the only way to truly move forward.

A deep breath escaped Nolan's mouth. He felt a sense of relief. His mind stopped racing and the bubbles in his stomach begun to settle. "It's so good to hear you say that, baby. To tell you the truth, that's all I really want now. I really want us to be a real family; just as you've been saying all this time. I realized that now, and I just hope it's not too late."

Satin's leg begun to shake in a mild manner as her thoughts raced. She had become frustrated with the anticipation of not knowing. "Nolan, just tell me. What is it that you need to talk to me about?"

"Satin, I haven't been really faithful to you," Nolan outed as he put his head down in premeditated guilt.

Satin took a deep breath, held the air in her lungs and slowly exhaled. She knew that much already, but was grateful that Nolan somehow found it in himself to finally come clean of his infidelity, something she already suspected. Satin was beyond ready to stop playing the guessing game with herself; backspace, wondering why Nolan was never home with her and Noah. She decided it was time to put the long-lived worries to death.

"Nolan, I know you haven't. I told you that much already the other night. A blind woman could see that you were cheating on me; you're never here. I know you must think I'm some kind of fool, and that's why you continue to treat me the way that you do. This all needs to stop, Nolan. I don't think I can take much more of your cheating; in fact, I know I can't. I wasn't raised that way," Satin said with sincerity.

Nolan knew he was fucking up big time, and if he didn't get his act together, he could possibly lose Satin forever. Nolan knew he had a good girl in his life who was willing to stay with him no matter what he may have done in the past. But, Nolan also realized that his time was running out, and if he wanted to keep his family, he needed to make some major changes. Nolan was a little boy trying to fill a grown man's shoes. Something his own daddy didn't have the courage to do.

"No baby, I don't think you're a fool. I know that you love me, and want to do what is best for our son, and for us, too. Them hoes out there ain't half the woman that you are. I was just too stupid to see it at the time."

"I do want to do what's best for our son. He needs you, Nolan. You're the only man that's a part of his life. I'm a female, I can't possibly raise a male all on my own. I can raise Noah, but I can't teach him the things a daddy can teach his son. Potty training Noah was challenging with him being a boy in all. I don't stand when I pee, I sit, and you taught him that. I come from a two-parent household, Nolan, and I just want to do what's best for our son."

"I know you do, and I'm sorry I've taking you for granted. Man… I was stupid. I have everything I want and need right here with you and our son."

With every nice thing, Nolan uttered, Satin's heart filled with joy. She and Nolan finally had a conversation that Satin had been waiting to have for three years. She believed Nolan had finally saw the light and had come around to wanting the same as she wanted. Satin convinced herself that her waiting for Nolan was not in vain and that all was not lost. She could save her family and finally be happy.

"So, this is what Mrs. Karen was talking about? Did you go over there and speak to her about it first? You know… Mrs. Karen is a really good person. I trust her as if she was my very own mother. I know she loves our son, and I believe she loves me too. She wants to do nothing more but to help us, Nolan. You should really take some time out and get to know her. You'll see what I'm talking about, you'll see."

Nolan grabbed Satin by the hand. He hated to disappoint her now that they had reached an understanding, but Nolan knew he had to tell Satin the full truth, or the woman she just told him that she trusted and loved like her own mother would tell Satin herself. Nolan never feared losing Satin until that day. He knew he had her wrapped around his finger, but the tie was on the verge of loosening. Nolan did not want to lose; it wasn't in his nature as a man; even if winning didn't ultimately change him in the end.

"Satin, Mrs. Karen came over while you were at work today."

"I know; she came over to get Noah's favorite toy. You know how that boy acts if he doesn't have the *Incredible Hulk*. She called me at work and told me Noah was cutting up for his toy, and I asked her to come over and get it. Wait a minute, how did you know she came over? I never called you to tell you."

"No, you didn't. I know because I was here."

"You were? That's right, you did say you got off early today. Oh wait, you got laid off and that's why you were here? Oh baby, I'm so sorry that happened. I…"

Nolan interrupted Satin, "Satin, no, I didn't get laid off. I left work early," he spoke.

Nolan was also getting impatient with what he had to say. He was ready to say it and get it over with. He was ready to be done with that conversation and work towards being there for Satin and Noah.

"Okay, so you left work early. What's the big deal?"

"While I was here, and as I said, Mrs. Karen came over. When she did, I wasn't alone."

"You weren't?" Satin looked confused. "So, who were you with then?"

"A girl… but I ended things today, and she will no longer be an interference between us. I meant what I said, baby. I want my family, and I'm willing to do whatever it takes to keep you and Nolan in my life." Satin quickly removed her hand from Nolan's. Her heart skipped several beats and palpitated in her chest. Her breathing grew brash and mind started racing.

Satin slowly raised from the sofa and stood up. She started to slowly back away from Nolan. She placed her hand firmly on her chest to try and calm its rhythm, but Satin's nerves were shot to hell and body started to tremble. Satin's trembling hands were so uncontrollable, that if she held on to a glass, it would have fallen and shattered. Satin had a hard time grasping what Nolan had just said to her.

Nolan stood up. "Baby, baby… are you okay?" he asked as he slowly paced toward Satin.

"STOP! NO…NO…NO… You did not have a girl in my home, Nolan! Tell me you did not bring another woman to my home where I pay majority of the bills for you and our son!"

"Satin, baby, please just listen…"

"SHUT UP, NOLAN! SHUT THE FUCK UP!" Satin yelled as she used vulgar profanity, which was something Satin wouldn't normally do because it wasn't spoken in her home as a child. The word fuck just slipped out of Satin's vocabulary unexpectedly and for good reason.

"Satin! I thought you said we could get through whatever it was I had to tell you? If I knew you would react like this, I would have followed my first mind, and just packed my shit and left without any explanation as to why. Nigga is trying to be honest with you, and you overreacting, bruh. You're overreacting and need to chill, man."

"OVERREACTING! OVERREACTING, MY ASS! What else happened, huh? What else happened, Nolan, while you had some girl in my apartment while I was at work? WHAT ELSE HAPPENED!" Satin yelled so loudly that the neighbors could hear her behind the walls.

Karen heard the two of them arguing, but didn't want to cause any more trouble, so she decided to keep her distance. She knew Satin was okay because she could hear her hollering and screaming through the door.

"I don't know if I should even get all into that, man. You already acting an ass."

"I'm acting an ass?! You had a girl in the apartment where I LAY MY HEAD. Mind you… this is MY SHIT! I invited YOU here to stay with me and your son, not the other way around, Nolan. You will get into what else, or I'll just go get the rest from Mrs. Karen."

Satin begun to walk off. Nolan grabbed her by the forearm and she threw punches his way. "LET ME GO! I'm tired of your shit, Nolan! I'm too good to you. I have done everything to try and keep you in our son's life, and this is how you REPAY ME?!"

Satin continued to hit at Nolan. His body didn't move as quickly as his brain. Satin's tightly balled fist met the side of Nolan's jaw. She got a good strike right on his cheekbone. Nolan was light skinned, so Satin's hit caused his face to bruise.

"Satin! Calm your ass down, man! Don't do that shit again. I'm sure all the neighbors hear you. Chill the fuck out, man."

"REALLY, NOLAN?! You weren't worried about the neighbors when you had some BITCH in my apartment, and NOWWW you all worried. FUCK THAT! I'll RAISE MY VOICE IF I WANT TO! THIS IS MY SHIT!" Satin shouted as she became the one to lose all self-control.

Nolan just stared at Satin. He didn't know what to do with her, she was showing a different side from the coy timid young girl he met at the church. Satin revealed a side of herself Nolan had never seen before. Timid Satin had gone away in hiding, and had no intentions of ever returning after that experience. The Satin that stood before Nolan he didn't recognize. He was confused and didn't know what else to expect or do.

Nolan knew he was wrong, and was trying to be mindful that he was the one to cause the commotion. He really didn't want to make matters worse. He calmed himself down and spoke in a still tone.

"Baby..."

"Don't you baby me, Nolan. Don't baby me!" Satin pointed her finger at Nolan.

"Okay, okay, Satin. Will you please just calm down so we can finish talking about this like two civilized adults? I ain't going nowhere baby... I mean, Satin. I'm here. WE have all night to talk about this, but I'm going to need you to calm down. The both of us getting all upset won't solve anything."

Satin paced the floor. She had never been that upset in all her twenty years of existing. Not even Bishop's abandonment upset her that much. Sure, Satin was hurt by her father, but even that didn't send fire though her veins like Nolan's betrayal had done. Nolan's betrayal bruised the parts of Satin that a father would never understand.

To be a daughter was one thing, but to be a woman was a whole other ordeal. Satin wasn't any different than any other woman, older or younger. It killed her emotionally to find out that the man she had been involved with was involved with another woman and sexually, at that. That was the side of Satin that Nolan got to damage. At first, she was willing to let go of Nolan's mishaps, but he had taken it to another level. One that she didn't see coming.

"What else happened, Nolan? What else happened? Tell me before I go ask Mrs. Karen, because now that I think about it, I'm sure she knows the whole story because she tried to warn me. But I guess Mrs. Karen wanted you to be man enough and tell me yourself. Soo... what happened? What else happened, Nolan?"

"Are you calm?"

"Yes... I am calm. What happened?" Satin interrogated in a calmer tone but continued to crush the floor with her shoes.

"I um... I don't know."

"Oh yes, you know. Don't play with me, Nolan. My patience is already shot, tell me what else happened, pleeeease for the love of God?"

"Man, I didn't even know you gave that woman a key."

Satin gave Nolan an evil stare, and then he knew if he didn't finish the story, she would run out the door and get the rest of his story of infidelity from Mrs. Karen as she had already threatened.

Nolan continued, "I um... Mrs. Karen walked down on me and the girl having sex," he finally spilled.

Satin's mouth dropped open, her heart sunk again and knees became weak. The unstableness in her knees commanded Satin down to the floor. Satin's chin sunk in her chest and she cried like a baby. Satin thought about all the times she cried that Nolan was not home with her and Noah. Satin reflected on how many times she felt as though she was not good enough for him, and that was the reason why he didn't want to commit to her. Satin also thought about Nolan abandoning her when she was pregnant with Noah, and all the nights she cried and prayed when she was homeless, living in the shelter that he would somehow come saved them.

Satin thought about Bishop and his abandonment, and her mother who she secretly felt should have done more to make him let her stay. Satin's whole life played back in her head. It was like she had pressed the rewind button and couldn't fast forward or press stop all together.

"I'm so sorry, baby. I really am. I'm so sorry for everything I have ever done to you and our son. I know now that I was wrong. I know that now. Remember… we both are young and must figure things out along the way. I was only eighteen when you became pregnant. I didn't know how to be a father, so I ran. I was scared, Satin. I never had a father around and I didn't know what one should be like. I never had a playbook for father's nor did I have an instruction manual. When you came to me and asked me to move in here, everything in me wanted to say no, but I thought it was time that I stepped up to the plate, so I did. I'm not going to even justify my actions; they were fucked up. I see my mistakes now, and I want to make them up to you and Noah."

Satin allowed Nolan's plead to saturate her mind and heart. She then raised her head slowly, and with swollen eyes that were bloodshot red, she gazed at Nolan. Satin sniffed a few times to keep her nose that was filled with mucus, from crying so hard, from spilling onto her face.

Satin's head felt as though someone had knocked her over with a brick; it was throbbing like a toothache. She took in a few breaths and tried to calm herself down because she begun to feel sick. Satin's pressure was elevated due to the stress and didn't even know it. Any worse news would have sent her straight to the emergency room going into cardiac arrest.

In that moment, Satin knew what she had to do. She knew that Nolan would be the death of her at an early age if she didn't put a stop to his madness. Satin finally spoke.

"You mean to tell me... after everything I've done... everything I've done to try and keep us together for the sake of our son, this is the way you say thank you? I invite you into my home, and you bring a girl in here, my home, my bed and have sex with her? Really, Nolan?'

Satin begun to rock slowly to try and calm her anxiety and anger down as the words that rolled off her tongue begun to upset her all over again.

"Baby..." Nolan started but remembered Satin had already warmed him to stop referring to her as baby. "I mean, Satin. I know that I was wrong, I take full responsibility for my actions. I'm just stepping up and being a man and asking for another chance. One more chance, baby? I mean Satin. One more..."

Before Nolan could finish the statement, Satin interrupted him. She took everything, and found the last ounce of strength she had left in her body and stood up to her feet.

"You are all out of chances, we are DONE! Get your shit and GET OUT!" Satin yelled and pointed to the door. She realized in that moment, Nolan was who he was and there was no changing that. Another woman in her home was the straw that broke the camel's back. Satin couldn't fathom looking at the father of her child: she wanted nothing more to do with him.

"Hey, now... I said I'm sorry. WE are not done! I live here too, I paid bills here too, and I ain't going nowhere!" Nolan boomed as he walked close to Satin and tried to intimidate her with the sound of his voice and masculine energy.

Satin reached on the side on the desk of the computer, and grabbed the medal, heavy duty hole puncher. Something wicked invaded her thoughts and burned through her entire body. Before Satin knew it, she had whacked Nolan across the forehead. Nolan stumbled back and dropped to the floor. Satin immediately realized what she had done and gasped as she grabbed her mouth as the hole puncher hit the floor.

Satin looked at Nolan and realized he wasn't breathing. Her legs couldn't move, neither did her brain. She was stuck and went into shock.

Chapter Seventeen

Every Dog Has Its Day

Satin snapped out of her state of bewilderment and fell to the floor. She looked at Nolan and didn't catch sight of his chest moving up and down from breathing. She called out Nolan's name a few times, and he did not answer. Satin's panicked emotions went into high gear; she didn't know what to do. Her thoughts screamed move, move, but her body could not pick up the signals.

Finally, Satin crawled to the front door, and used the doorknob to give her balance. She struggled to raise from the floor, but made it by the grace of God. She glanced back at Nolan and ran across the hall. She pounded on the door with her fist and prayed that Karen would open. Karen heard the pounding and powerwalked to the living room from the kitchen. She opened the door and noticed Satin shaking in her boots and appearing to be scared.

"What is it, sweetheart? Are you okay, is everything okay" Karen asked with worried eyes.

Satin stared at Karen and couldn't fathom the words to let Karen know what she had just done to Nolan. Satin could hear the sound of her own heartbeat from inside of her eardrum. The pounding in Satin's chest intensified; she struggled to control her nerves as her body shook like a vintage alarm clock with bells that wouldn't stop going off until someone pressed the stop button.

"I killed, him. I think I killed Nolan."

Karen gasped. She stepped outside the door and walked away from Satin. She peeked through Satin's opened door and noticed Nolan lying on the floor. Karen saw that Nolan was not dead because he moved one of his feet. Karen inhaled and exhaled; she took in deep breaths, as a sign of relief came over her. She turned around and walked back over to Satin standing in her doorway, looking like a scared little girl.

Karen took Satin by the hand and escorted her inside of her apartment.

"Sit right here. Nolan is not dead, thank God. I saw him move, but I need you to stay right here with Noah, okay? I need you to calm down and take deep breaths."

Karen walked to the kitchen, grabbed a bottle of water and went back into the living room. She handed Satin the water and she took it.

"He's alive, are you sure?" Satin asked as her hand still trembled as she attempted to open the water.

"Yes, Nolan's alive, I'm sure of it. When I peeked in, I saw him move his feet. He probably has a concussion. Did you hit him over the head?"

"Yes, I believe that's where I hit him, but I'm not sure. It all happened so fast."

"Okay, it's okay. Stay with Noah, he's sitting in the kitchen watching TV. We were eating cake. I'm going see about his dad, you stay here, okay?"

"Okay," Satin agreed.

Karen walked out of her apartment and back over to Satin's. She noticed Nolan sitting on the couch, a bit disoriented and holding his head while squeezing his eyes shut.

Karen left out of the apartment again, went back into her refrigerator and grabbed an ice pack. She was even on edge because of the current events that had taken place with Nolan earlier that day to the time Satin nearly killed him. A part of Karen felt guilty. She started to feel as though she probably should have just walked out of the apartment when she realized Nolan was in the bedroom with another girl.

"Is he okay?" Satin asked with a worried expression.

"Yes, he's fine. Just a bump on the head, that's all. I'm sure, Nolan will be fine once he puts this on his head."

"Where is little Darrius?"

"He's gone home."

Satin continued to feed Noah his cake and Karen walked back to Satin's apartment. Nolan noticed Karen and jumped up. "Where that bitch at? Imma kill her ass!" Nolan yelled, still holding his head.

"You won't do no such thing, young man. Look at you, you can barely even stand. Now, take this ice pack and put it on your head, and sit down before you fall over and hit your head again."

Karen reached the pack to Nolan. He knocked it out of her hand. "I don't want that shit! I don't want anything from you. It's all your fault! If you would have minded your own motherfucking business none of this would have happened."

Karen hauled off and slapped the taste out of Nolan's mouth. Nolan grabbed his face and raised up to Karen, gawking her in the eyes with balled fist as dragon fire left his mouth in form of air.

"You better calm yourself down, young man. I'm no Satin, and I have a son damn near twice your age. You will not talk to me like that, ever. Do you understand me?" Karen spoke in an aggressive tone. She did not fear Nolan, and had every intention of letting him know that.

"Lady, if you ever put your hands on me again, I will forget your ass is old and show you what niggas like me do to old bitches like you. Do you understand me?!" Nolan returned the aggression. He was beyond angry and wanted to kill somebody or something.

"Oh yeah, try me if you want to. You think you bad? See, let me tell you the difference between you and me. I know who fight my battles for me, do you? You want to act all hard and mad when you're the one around here causing all the trouble. You want to blame everyone else but yourself for what you've done. You messed over a good girl, not the other way around. You better check yourself son, before you wreck yourself. Go on and get your things and get on out of here. That's the least you can do for your son and the mother of your child, who takes damn good care of him and loves him with every breath in her body. Go on, get on out of here and leave this girl alone. You done caused enough trouble in her life, don't you think?"

Nolan looked at Karen. He was pissed as hell, but knew she was right. He could not find one word in his vocabulary that would disagree with what Karen spoke to him.

Nolan slowly backed off, walked to the bedroom, grabbed a couple things of his and put them inside a duffel bag. He sat on the bed for a second and considered everything he did to Satin, even leaving her when she was pregnant.

After drowning in his own self-pity, Nolan stood up and walked back to the living room.

"Listen, I'm sorry for disrespecting you. You are older than my momma, and she really wouldn't be happy with me if she were to find out I talked to an elderly lady the way I've talked to you. Will you please tell Satin I really am sorry, and I'll be back to get the rest of my things another time?"

Karen gently smiled at Nolan. She wanted him to know that she had calmed down too.

"Only if you take this ice pack," She reached the pack to Nolan again and he grabbed it. "I forgive you, young man, and I accept and appreciate your apology. God has a plan for all of us and that includes you, too. I will tell Satin what you said. As for Noah, try not to worry yourself so much about him, he'll be okay. He has a mother who would walk to the ends of the earth and back to protect him. I truly believe you know that already. Take some time and get yourself together. Who knows what the future holds for you and the mother of your child. Only God knows that and I'm the last to judge anyone."

Nolan looked at Karen and a tear escaped his eyes. He knew Karen was coming from a good place to speak to him the way she did after everything that he done that day. Nolan knew there were not many people like Karen in the world; he recognized that and the light that shined so bright in Karen's eyes when she spoke about the goodness of God. Nolan also knew Satin had a good person looking out for her and Noah right next door and that gave him comfort.

Nolan left.

*****

Satin sat over at Karen's, because she didn't want to go home after the night she had, Karen invited her and Noah to spend a night.

Sebastian was at his home kicked back, downing Heinekens with his homeboy, Rome. The two guys watched the game and talked about Sebastian's recent alleged involvement with the robbery at the bank. Rome was the one who went over to check on him after being left at the altar.

Sebastian hadn't spoken to Satin since earlier that day at work; he thought about texting her, but didn't want to be pushy. Satin appeared as though she needed space after the conversation they had at lunch two weeks prior, and Sebastian convinced himself to believe that space was what he would give to her.

Sebastian was a considerate man, he only wanted to do what he thought was best for Satin and not himself, no matter how much he missed hearing her voice. Sebastian desired to talk to Satin, though. He thought about how much he enjoyed being in her presence, and was becoming very fond of their friendship, but wasn't going to press the issue.

Sebastian and Rome ate take out, hot wings and were drinking beer in the theater room as Rome puffed off his blunt.

"Dogg, that shit is mad crazy. How could you work with niggas who are basically accusing you of stealing? Dogg... I don't see how you do it, I'll be mugging them niggas all day, hoping they say something out of pocket so I could beat the brakes off their asses. You want to hit this?" Rome reached the blunt to Sebastian.

"Naw money, I'm good and that's what they want me to do. That only would prove them right. I refuse to give them hating ass white folks that satisfaction. I'm playing nice for now, but know that, I have my attorney cocked and ready, because as soon as this bullshit investigation is over, I'm going to hit their ass with a lawsuit for slander. You gotta hit them white folks where it hurts the most, in their motherfucking pockets. That's how you beat them at their own game, you feel me?"

"I feel ya, my nigga. Better you than me though dogg, that shit is crazy," Rome spoke as he finished his smoke and picked up a wing and cleaned it to the bone.

"Who you telling. I'm just glad I'm not like I used to be, dogg. Being a hot head got me into too much shit as it is. I can't let that side of Sebastian resurface. Them niggas ain't ready."

"That's the problem, this new Sebastian done got all politically correct and shit; unleash the beast, my nigga," Rome teased. "I'm still tripping on the fact that ole girl pulled that shit at the wedding though, dogg. Nigga, when I came over that day, you were fucked up, my nigga. You were drunk as a fucken skunk and wanted to fight me and everything. I was like...yo nigga, you trippin'. I ain't the one who fucked you over. Nigga, sober the fuck up."

Sebastian slightly laughed. "I'm sorry bout' that, dogg. I mean... most of that shit I don't even remember, so don't remind me," Sebastian joked as he ate a couple of hot wings.

"My bad money, that shit just tripped me the fuck out. I never saw you not in control. You always were the one to be in control, even when you were whipping nigga's asses, you still were in control," Rome joked.

"Bet," Sebastian agreed. "I don't know man, I'm just doing what I can to try and put the pieces back together, know what I mean?"

"Yeah dogg, I know exactly what you mean. Females really think us men don't have feelings and shit. We hurt too, but once I get over a bitch, she can't do nothing for me but suck my dick."

"Nigga, you wild," Sebastian chortled. "Naw money, she can't even do that for me. I want nothing more to do with Angie's ass. I'm done," Sebastian spoke as he dusted his hands and wiped the excess spicy sauce off with a napkin.

Sebastian reached for his beer and drunk half of the bottle to equalize the burning sensation in his mouth from the hot wings. He sat the bottle in the chair's cup holder.

"So, you mean to tell me if Angie came over here right now and offered to suck your dick, you wouldn't let her?"

"Naw nigga, I wouldn't," Sebastian affirmed.

Rome looked at him as if he were crazy.

"Aight nigga you got me, fuck yeah, I'll let her break a nigga off!"

Sebastian and Rome burst into laughter.

"Nigga, I know you would. Niggas let crackheads suck their dicks, so I know you ain't 'bout to turn down a pretty woman like Angela who wants to give you brain."

"Man, I'm done talking 'bout Angela's ass. I'm trying to make her ass not so much as an afterthought, and soon, hopefully not a thought at all." *Some head would have been good the other night when she came, but nigga aint playin' no games with her ass. Damn... this nigga in here reminding me how good that shit feels. I gotta run in something soon.*

"I feel you, my nigga. I don't blame you though, dogg. She just doesn't know, she had one of the good ones compared to myself and what your ass used to be. See-- that's why I dog them hoes out. Them hoes aint loyal for real, dogg."

"Man, didn't I tell yo ass I'm done talking about women. I'm trying to get back into this game, bruh."

"I told you yo ass was getting soft, nigga. Since when did a nigga from the street don't want to talk about bitches?"

"Since right now, nigga!" Sebastian joked and turned up the volume to the game.

Rome laughed. He and Sebastian didn't hang out as much as they did when they were younger and had run the streets of

California. Rome still hadn't gotten quite used to the white-collar Sebastian that worked for the government. Rome was having a hard time believing Sebastian had put all his thug ways in a safe box and threw away the key.

"Ay nigga, aight, I'm done talking 'bout bitches, but let me ask you something."

"Damn nigga, yo ass doing a lot of chick chattin'! Wassup?"

"Naw man, I'm just kicking it with my nigga, my ace. You know, we really didn't hang out much since you were all in love and shit. But naw nigga, just glad to see you bouncing back, that's all. I was kind of worried 'bout you, nigga."

"I'm good, money. The shit hurts, but ain't nothing I can do about that. I'm aight though. I'll survive."

"I dig that. Ay… about that robbery, though. Do they have any clue as to who the niggas were? I mean… I know you said they think one was you, but what about the other?"

"Naw, I don't think they do, because if they did, his ass would be in jail."

"True dat. That shit is crazy though. Niggas out here just don't give a fuck. I didn't think real niggas was still doing that shit. All the free money in them streets, why risk your freedom running in a motherfucking bank with cameras and witnesses at shit?"

"Right. I don't know man, the cameras don't give much but a height and possible race, considering what it shows surrounding the eyes and mouth of the mask. Peep this though… the nigga who supposedly is me went in the safe and walked out with five million."

"Damn, that nigga paid."

"For now, I guess. He better put that shit somewhere safe because he definitely going to need it for an attorney."

"So how did ole boy even know the combination? I mean… they are locked with combinations, right?"

"Yeah, they are and that's why I'm being investigated. The dude had the combination. The cameras show him unlocking it with ease, without even looking on a piece of paper or anything. That's how they know it was an inside job, and since Dude appeared to be a young black male, my build and height, now I'm a suspect. If you ask me, it could have been any of them dudes who work there. On some real shit, they could be setting me up and hired somebody to do it. One thing about the elite… no amount money would ever be enough. Them niggas money hungry as fuck and power struck. Them niggas never satisfied."

"Damn, that's cold, bruh."

"You damn right it's cold, but nigga aint even worried. Maybe a little bit because my reputation is on the line, but I know I didn't do it and they cannot prove I did something that I did not do."

"I surely hope you right, for your sake, dogg. That would be really fucked up if you were to go down for something you did not do."

"I won't. They can't prove shit. Like I said, I didn't do shit to begin with, so what are they going to prove?

*****

Sebastian and Rome continued to run it and watch the basketball game. A couple of hours later, Rome left to go be with one of his side chicks. Sebastian showered and went into his bedroom. He watched a little more television before his heavy eyes caught up to him; Sebastian dozed off. Not even five minutes into his slumber, the phone rung and he answered.

"Hey, you. I wasn't expecting to hear from you. What's up?" Sebastian asked in a sluggish tone.

Satin lightly snickered. "Is that, right? I'm sorry if I woke, you. Were you asleep?"

"Yup, just dozed off, but you good. What you doing?"

"Parked outside in your driveway."

Sebastian was shaken by Satin's remark and rose from the bed; he sat up with his back against the headboard. He was confused because he thought Satin wanted space, but yet he flirted with the idea. "You are?"

"Yes, I am. I hope you don't have any company, but if so, I'm sorry, I'll just leave and see you tomorrow at work."

"Your hard headed, aren't you? I told you that you were good. I don't have any company, but I guess I do now, right?"

Sebastian stepped out the bed and skimmed the room for his basketball shorts. He noticed them on a small pile on a chair. He fetched the shorts, put the phone between his ear and shoulder and slipped into his shorts.

"I guess you do," Satin playfully teased. *Why are you breathing so hard? What are you doing in there?*

Sebastian left his bedroom and jogged down the stairs. He went to the door, opened it, and Satin was standing in front of the doorway looking like a breath of fresh air. Sebastian's chest was bare. His muscles appeared as though he just had a vigorous work out; he was ripped in all the right places. He noticed Satin's hungry eyes peering at his rib cage before she raised her head and finally stared him in the eyes.

Damn... you are so fine. I'm still having a hard time believing that woman didn't want all that I see before me, Satin thought to herself.

I see you looking, the thought swept across Sebastian's mind as he gloated on the inside.

"Uhhh... I'm sorry about the shirt. I was actually naked, but I did put some shorts on for you; just for you," he jested.

Maybe this time you could have kept them off. "Ummm... I've noticed," Satin returned the tease.

"Come on in here, with your bad self," Sebastian reimbursed the humor as he recognized Satin's eyes staring at his dick, which appeared as though it was erect, but wasn't.

After Satin stepped inside of Sebastian's home, he closed the door behind the two of them and she followed him into the living room. Sebastian walked to the kitchen and Satin followed him there as well. He opened the refrigerator and grabbed a bottle of water.

"Would you like something to drink?"

"Naw, I'm good," Satin stood, watching him.

She couldn't take her eyes off Sebastian. After her unbelievable night with Nolan, it was uplifting to be in the company of someone she admired and obviously crushed on. Satin's eyes were no longer swollen. After Karen gave her something for the puffiness, they appeared as though she had never drowned herself in sorrow earlier that evening. Satin was still overwhelmed with hurt and betrayal, but tried to put a smile on her face and what had happened to the back of her memory.

"So, what are you doing here, baby girl? Where yo' man at?" Sebastian went straight in for the kill.

"Geezzz, one question at a time," Satin teased.

"Okay, well I'll start with the first one. What are you doing here?"

"I just so happened to be in the neighborhood," Satin joked and Sebastian looked at her and knew that she was pestering him.

Satin grabbed a seat at the countertop. Sebastian kept standing and wet his throat with a sip of water.

"I don't know what I'm doing here to tell you the truth. I um… I was over by Mrs. Karen's, the woman who babysits my son, and I went home to shower and had every intention of going back over there, but on my way across the hall, I found myself in the car driving instead, so here I am."

Sebastian continued to observe Satin. "Interesting," he one worded her.

Sebastian didn't want to force the conversation. He figured if Satin wanted to share something with him, she would, all on her own. He didn't want to scare her off like he did that day at the restaurant. He learned that he had to ease things in with Satin; too much all at once made her very uncomfortable.

Satin's head slipped to her chest as a sudden flashback of what happened between her and Nolan crept into her thoughts. She raised her head and Sebastian's keen gaze met her eyes, as if he was waiting for Satin to return her attention back to him.

"To answer the second part of your question, Nolan and I, my son's daddy that is, we got into it really hot and heavy tonight.

He moved out," Satin dropped her head again, still not totally convinced that her and Noah would be fine without Nolan after everything that transpired that day.

Sebastian walked closer to Satin. He placed his hand on Satin's chin and slowly lifted her head and gawked deep into her eyes.

"Are you okay, did he hit you?" he asked with a penetrating gaze.

Sebastian could no longer not asked questions. He needed to know that Satin was okay.

Satin shook her head no, but her eyes begun to water, although she had tried her damndest to fight back the tears.

Sebastian noticed the inward struggle and took Satin by the hand. She slid off the bar stool and he escorted Satin to the living room. Sebastian stood in front the couch and Satin took a seat on the sofa as he decided to sit next to her.

"Hey, are you sure you're okay; how can I help?" Sebastian placed a hand on Satin's knee cap.

One tear escaped Satin's eyes. She brushed her cheek with her hand to rid her face of the teardrop. "This is becoming quite regular, isn't it? I'm so embarrassed, and sorry, that I have been this emotional lately. For some reason or another, really emotional around you. I told myself I wasn't going to cry again, and yet here I am crying." Satin shook her head in disappointment.

"It's okay, Satin. It's really okay that you show your emotions around me. You don't have to be sorry, you didn't do anything wrong. I don't see you no different now than when your laughing. I just see a woman who's going through something tough in her life. I think vulnerability is sexy in a woman, quite frankly. I know this can't be easy for you or your son either, for that matter. Where is he, by the way?"

"Um... he's okay. I left Noah sleeping in the bed by Mrs. Karen. I was supposed to stay over as well, but I went home to shower and as I said, I ended up here."

"For what it's worth, I'm glad that you came. So, are you going to tell me what happened between the two of you?" Sebastian asked with gentle eyes and a sincere heart.

He felt compelled to know what had gotten Satin all gloomy, so much so that she ended up coming over to his place. Sebastian didn't mind that Satin had come over, but he was curious to know why.

"Where do you want me to begin? What didn't happen between us," Satin dropped her head to her chest again, feeling ashamed that she was a part of the baby daddy troubles committee.

Satin didn't ask for her newfound young black single motherhood and would have given anything to reverse the outcome for Noah's sake. Sebastian cuffed Satin's chin with his palm and tenderly raised her face. He waited for Satin to look at him before he spoke. Satin's eyes finally fell on Sebastian and he begun to express his feelings.

"You can start where ever you feel comfortable. I'm not going anywhere; we have all night."

Satin had begun to appreciate Sebastian more and more. A trivial smile swept across her down in the dumps face. Sebastian's caring personality caressed Satin's heart. She had never met a guy who cared the way that Sebastian did, and the fact that it came natural for him like a second nature. She knew Sebastian wasn't putting on a show just for her, it was just who he was.

Sebastian was someone who seemed to always have Satin's best interest at heart, and he unintentionally was stealing that same heart without notice. Satin valued Sebastian's opinion more and more, and saw someone she could learn to trust. Far more than she ever had with the man who she laid down with and bared a child.

"He called himself confessing his sins, I guess."

"So, there was no physical altercation?" Sebastian pressed.

He was worried that Satin was withholding some information. Sebastian was a straight shooter and his skepticism of Nolan had multiplied since Satin shared with him that Nolan raped her. Sebastian wanted to get to the point and get to it quick.

"Let me just put this out there. Nolan only got physical with me one time. I do know that no means no, and I'm not justifying his actions. Honestly, that was the first and only time that something like that ever happened." Satin felt the need to defend Nolan's poor actions.

"Satin, I don't know if you are aware of this, but take this for what it's worth. No matter if it only happened one time, it only takes one time, and if you disregard a woman abuser's actions, or stay with a man like that, I guarantee you that it would happen again."

Satin was left speechless and realized Sebastian wasn't speaking from a place of malice, but truth instead. One that she needed to hear. Satin agreed with him wholeheartedly; she just hated the fact that Sebastian saw her in the light of an abused woman.

Satin was naïve to believe that Nolan's heart was ever in the right place. He showed his true colors from the time she met him, but somehow Satin expected something different from a young boy who was not ready to fully take responsibility for his actions of fathering a child. Satin had faith that they both would quickly mature and do the right thing for the sake of Noah.

"Sebastian, I don't want you to think that I don't take what he did seriously, because believe me I do, I just don't accept the term that I'm an abused woman, because I'm not."

"And you shouldn't. Your situation does not define who you are. I don't view you as a helpless, defenseless, abused woman, if that's what you're thinking. I'm just merely making an observation, that's all. You can take what you want from it, and leave what does not apply. Only you know what's best for you ultimately, Satin. I only hope that you just don't lessen what was done, and call it what it was, that's it."

"And I do, believe me. I have a very hard time even forgetting it. Well, I don't have to worry about Nolan anymore anyway because as I've said he left."

"Did he just leave on his own?"

"No, I asked him to leave. He confessed to me that my neighbor, who lives across the hall, the woman who babysits our son, walked in on him and some girl having sex in my apartment where I lay my head, the same apartment that I invited him to move into with me and our son, mind you. The NERVE of him."

Sebastian's eyes darted, damn near popping out of the sockets. He knew as a man Satin had to be dealing with a bonehead after she told him what Nolan had done. Sebastian was surprised to find out that he had gone that far. Sebastian wasn't a Saint, but he had no respect for Nolan and didn't mind expressing that to Satin.

"Man, you have got to be kidding me. I mean how… and why, would he think that was okay? I swear, some of these dudes make it bad for men like me. That's the kind of shit that only a cold hearted, low down ass dirty nigga would do. Man… that's crazy."

Satin kept quiet.

"Hey, I know this is easier said than done, but he did you a favor. Not breaking your heart though, that's not what I meant, but Dude allowed you to see him for who he really was, a sorry punk ass nigga. You're better off without Dude if you ask me, you and your son."

Satin continued to keep quiet. She had the same look on her face that she had at the restaurant. Sebastian knew he was pushing the envelope, but wanted to make his stance perfectly clear to Satin.

"Listen baby girl, I know the two of you share a child together and everything, and unfortunately, you will still have to deal with him on some level. I'm just sorry that you have to go through all of this, I really am. I wish there was more I could do to make you feel better," Sebastian continued.

Sebastian's heart begun to carry pure empathy for the young woman who cared for him in his time of need. He wished he could turn the nice sentiment in some equivalent way, form or fashion.

"There is," Satin replied as she stared into Sebastian's earnest eyes.

Sebastian tried to read through Satin's remark and her body language without jumping the gun. She scooted her petite body closer to him and continued to stare. Sebastian's muscled frame had awakened Satin's womanhood and she liked the way it made her feel. Satin could no longer fight back her attraction to Sebastian and he could no longer fight his. They had begun to feel an emotional bond for one another.

"There is? What do you suggest?" Sebastian asked, not certain what Satin wanted from him, but had a pretty good idea because she had a seductive look in her eyes. Sebastian wanted to make sure they were on the same page before he made a move.

"You could kiss me," Satin softly whispered.

Sebastian continued to stare at Satin. He wanted to kiss her just as much as Satin wanted to kiss him, but also knew once those lines of friendship were crossed, there was no going back.

"Kiss you? Are you sure that's what you want, Satin?"

"Yes, I'm sure. That's exactly what I want you to do, Sebastian. I want you to kiss me, please," Satin confirmed.

Sebastian leaned in closer to Satin and examined her lovely, bronzed skin that was rich with melanin. He placed his palm on the side of Satin's face, leaned in and positioned his succulent lips on top of hers. Satin placed her hand on top of Sebastian's and opened her mouth to receive his tongue. Sebastian and Satin exchanged saliva and they both became emotionally and physically stimulated. They desired each other and Satin wanted nothing more but to have Sebastian deep inside of her brown sugar.

Sebastian leaned further in and pressed Satin to lean back on the couch. He slid between her legs as she opened them to give him a perfect fit. The two of them sucked, enticed and fondled each other on the couch until they both were hot and bothered. They exchanged heavy breathing and soft moans in each other mouths.

Sebastian rose from the couch and his manhood was standing at attention, a blind woman could see that he was more than ready to make love to Satin. She placed her hand on the stiff bulge that was outside of Sebastian's basketball shorts and tenderly fondled him.

That was something she wanted to do from the time he opened the door for her that night.

Sebastian closed his eyes and head dropped back. He pulled Satin up from the couch and escorted her upstairs into the bedroom. Soon as Satin and Sebastian hit the door, he started to kiss her again with fierce passion as they fell onto the pillow topped plush mattress. Sebastian raised Satin's leg so he could secure a perfect body to body, penis to vagina fit. He thought about all the sexual exciting things he wanted to do to Satin as his provocative thoughts motivated him.

Sebastian was ready to make Satin feel like a grown woman after he kissed her in all the places that mattered the most, but his conscious would not let him. He let go of Satin's leg, and sat up on the bed. Satin was left wondering where things went wrong.

"What's wrong, why did you stop?" she asked, full of confusion and hot as a jalapeno pepper.

"I can't do this man," Sebastian answered as his conscious spoke louder than his dick.

"So, we can't have sex?" Satin asked as she sat up from the bed.

"No, we can't, Satin. It wouldn't be fair to you. I'm fucked up man, and I don't want to take advantage of you being vulnerable right now."

"You're not taking advantage of me, this is what I want, Sebastian."

"No no baby girl, I can't, I just can't do this man. I won't do this to you. I would not be making love to you, Satin. I would be fucking you because the bitch who broke my heart still has it. You deserve more, more than I can give you right now."

"Let me decide what I deserve and what I don't deserve. I'm a grown woman, I am responsible for my own actions, not you. I don't know... maybe I just want to be fucked right now. Fucked by you, Sebastian."

Sebastian abruptly rose from the bed.

"I'm broken, Satin. Can't you see that? You deserve better baby girl. I'm angry on the inside all the time. I'm walking around at work with a chip on my shoulder. And get this one, I'm mad as fuck at that bitch for breaking my heart."

Sebastian's anger started to get the best of him. He turned around and hit the wall.

POW echoed through the room and shook Satin. Her eyes widened and her heart skipped a beat. She watched as Sebastian struggled to contain himself. Something inside of him quickly took over. He hated that Angela still affected him in more ways than he was willing to admit. His feelings for Angela did not disappear overnight, no more than they had formed overnight. It had only been a couple of months since the wedding and Sebastian was still hurt over what should have been.

"She used me! She got everything she could out of me until she was built up, just to return to him to be torn down again. I swear… sometimes I feel like I want to kill that bitch! I may not be as good as you think I am, Satin. I want to hurt a fucking woman, and I know I'm not that kind of man. I never put my hands on a woman EVER before, but I do want to strangle her ass to death. There… are you satisfied now? I'm a fucking monster, like every other nigga from the street."

Satin sat with everything Sebastian laid on her. She saw and felt his frustration, hurt and the anger that was caused from his previous relationship. Satin saw a broken man who was trying to get past his failed relationship and hurt.

Instead of taking Sebastian's words at face value, Satin sympathized with him. She did not blame Sebastian for feeling the way that he did towards the woman who broke his heart because she felt the same way about the man who had broken her heart. The Sebastian that she had gotten to know would never do the things that he spoke of doing to a woman.

Satin scooted closer to the end of the bed and stood up in front of Sebastian. She looked up to him and he gazed down at her. "I understand how you feel, and I don't blame you at all for being angry. I want this Sebastian, I really want and need to be with you right now."

Satin grabbed Sebastian by the hand. "I know you don't love me Sebastian, but I do believe you care. You're right, I do deserve better and when that time comes, I will get better. Right now, all that matters to me is that you care and that's enough for me. I know that sounds pretty pathetic, but I want to be with you Sebastian, I feel close to you and I know you feel close to me too."

Sebastian continued to stare in Satin's eyes. He thought long and thought hard.

"Okay, we can be together, but I don't want to hear shit from you when shit come up. I tried to warn you, but you won't listen. Okay, let's do it," Sebastian gave into Satin.

She was precious in Sebastian's eyes, and he wanted nothing more but to make her feel better after the night Satin had. If making love to her was what would do the trick, Sebastian was willing to do it, but only because Satin asked that of him.

Sebastian laid Satin back on the bed and started to kiss her. He removed her shirt, and then her pants. Satin begun to feel as though Sebastian had a point and she shouldn't be rushing him to do something he wasn't quite ready to do, because she felt as though she was ready. Her thoughts were running a mile a minute and she couldn't focus on what was about to happen between her and Sebastian. This was something that would ultimately change the dynamics of their friendship if it their relationship went sour, and Satin didn't want that to happen.

"Okay okay nooooo…. I don't want things to not be right between us," Satin stopped Sebastian just as he placed his head between her thighs.

Sebastian rolled over, scooted to the top and laid flat on his back with his hands tucked underneath the pillow. He gazed at the ceiling and didn't mumble one word.

"So, what now?" Satin asked.

"You wait for me."

"Wait for you?"

"Yes, wait for me. I don't want to break you in my brokenness, Satin. What if I break you? That's the last thing I want to do, I care about you. I don't want to bring you down with me, Satin. I don't want you to feel the pain and hurt that I feel inside."

Satin laid on her side and faced Sebastian as he continued to gaze into the ceiling.

"I am not in danger of being broken, because I already am," Satin spoke and Sebastian turned his attention to face her. "What if I'm the one who needs to be healed? What if I'm the one whose heart is broken so bad by a man, who only cared for me, because clearly it wasn't love. I was so naïve to believe that he wanted the same thing I wanted, which was to raise our son together. See… we always make things about us, this may not even be about you anymore. Have you even considered that? Maybe I'm the one who needs to know that I could still love after being broken down? Not only by a man, but also by my father, whom I trusted and still love to this day. I love my father unconditionally and not because of conditions. Will I ever step a foot back into my father's house after he put me out at seventeen years old because I was pregnant? No, but I will if he invites me back, because I love him and true love just doesn't go away because someone hurt us."

Sebastian turned on his side and he placed his hand on Satin's face and rubbed it as he gazed into her eyes. "I'm sorry, I didn't know that. You really have been through a lot, haven't you?"

Satin laid on Sebastian's chest. "You have no idea, that's only half of it."

"You can talk about it if you'd like, I told you I wasn't going anywhere and we have all night."

"I think we covered enough for one night. I'm exhausted, emotionally and physically. I really need to get back to Noah."

"I understand, and as I keep telling you, I'm here," Sebastian paused and the room was quiet. "Do you think I will ever love again?"

"Of course, you will. All things are possible with God."

"I don't believe in God. I used to, but not anymore."

Wait… what? How could anyone not believe in God? Satin thought to herself as she continued to lay in Sebastian's chest with eyes of terror.

Oh no, this may change everything.

Chapter Eighteen

Me and My House Will Serve God

Satin woke up in the bed with Noah sleeping comfortably in her chest. She thought about the night she had with Sebastian, and was lost as to where their friendship and potential relationship would go from there.

Satin was raised by a Pastor and God was all that was ever taught in her household. She knew an unevenly yoked relationship would never prosper; it just couldn't possibly work out. At least, that was what Satin was taught to believe.

Nolan was everything that Satin wasn't, but she knew Nolan believed in God because she met Nolan in the church. He was a member just as she was of her father's church, and stopped going just as she did once she became pregnant. Nolan was never a true Christian, Satin knew that, but was comfortable knowing that at least

Nolan knew that God did exist and he was saved by the blood of the lamb.

Satin hadn't believed in any other beliefs her entire life. The Christianity values, and way of thinking was all she ever knew and was deep rooted. Satin did not judge Sebastian for what he believed; she just couldn't understand that he did not believe that God even existed. Satin thought to herself how could a man have faith and hope in anything if he didn't have hope and faith in his creator?

Satin laid Noah in the middle of the bed, got up and went into the kitchen; looking for Karen. Karen was an early bird. It was barely six a.m. and she was up, drinking coffee and watching the early morning news.

"Good morning, Mrs. Karen."

"Good morning, sweetheart. I noticed you left out for a while last night, but I'm glad that you and Noah stayed over. I guess you found my keys on the rack in the kitchen, huh? Did you sleep well?"

"Yes, I slept well, thank you for having us. Yes, I found the keys. I didn't want to leave the door unlocked. I hope you don't mind."

"Not at all. I would have been worried had you not found them."

"I um… I just needed a breath of fresh air after everything that transpired, to tell you the truth."

"I would imagine you did, sugah plum. Just so you know, my door is always open to Noah, and to you as well."

"Thank you, and I can't truly thank you enough for everything that you have done for us. You are indeed a true gift from heaven. You are a blessing, not only in my little boy's life, but in mine as well," Satin said with sincerity.

"Ahhh… thank you, sugah. God is good and I have no problem whatsoever sharing his goodness."

Satin smiled. "I'm about to head on over to shower and get dressed for work. Noah is still sleeping, but I will take him with me and get him dressed as well. We will be back shortly."

"Where is Noah going?" Karen quipped with a look of concern on her face and raised eyebrows.

"Uhhh… nowhere really. He's staying here with you."

"Exactly, let that baby sleep. He's in his PJ's and he's quite comfortable. You go on and get ready for work. I'll dress Noah later if that will make you feel better," Karen sassed playfully.

"Okay, I'll just take his bag and put a change of clothing for the day and extra's just in case. I'll be sure to grab that toy as well. Mrs. Karen, I really don't want to put more on you with Noah. I really do have enough time to dress him myself."

"You are not putting anything on me, I volunteered. Now stop worrying so much about things that you really don't have to worry about, young lady. Putting clothes on a three-year-old who is going nowhere but across the hall from his own home is really not that big of a deal. You youngins', Mrs. Karen doesn't know what she's going to do with your tails."

"You're absolutely, right," Satin continued to smile. "I guess it doesn't make much sense to dress him."

"I have to preach that to my son and daughter in law all the time. They send my grandson here all dressed up like he's going to church somewhere. That's a waste of time dressing that boy, because as soon as they leave, I undress little Darrius all the time. I put him on the spare comfortable PJ's I have around here, and right before they come to pick him up in the evenings, I dress him back in his Sunday's best. My son always says, he doesn't know how I manage to keep him clean all day. Duhhh... silly boy. I undress him out of his best clothing, that's how. All he'll do is get them all dirty, playing and eating all day around here. Just doesn't make any sense at all."

Karen sipped her coffee. Satin smirked. She loved her some Karen. It reminded Satin that she needed to call her own mother to see how she had been doing after telling Satin that she hadn't been feeling well.

"Well, I'll head on home and I'll be back in a minute."

"Okay, sure. Darling?"

"Yes," Satin answered.

"Are you okay?" Karen asked with a face of worry.

After Karen noticed Satin had left her place, she didn't want to call Satin and seem like she wanted to invite herself into her business any more than she already was. Karen just got down on her knees, and asked God to give Satin the proper guidance she needed and to protect her and Noah from any more harm or danger.

"Uhh… yeah, sure, I'm okay," Satin answered with uncertainty. Her new reality had sat in overnight and she just wanted to focus on moving forward without Nolan.

"I know that you are going through a lot right now. Just know that God will take care of you and that baby, and everything else is in God's hand."

Satin peered at Karen with engaging eyes. "Yeah, I know. I just wish I could explain all of this to Noah when he starts asking for his daddy, that's all. When I left last night, I visited a really good friend of mine. Besides you, which I absolutely am grateful for, and know I couldn't do this without your help, he has also really been helping me through all of this. He's been nothing but caring and very understanding. I'm so glad that we are getting close. I mean, no not like that." Satin slightly tittered out of respect for Karen and what she thought of her mattered.

"Well, that's really good to know. At least you're surrounded by people who love and care about you. See… I told you. Look at God, he's working already," Karen rejoiced as she continued to drink her black coffee. *I just hope this young lady knows what she's doing, opening another door before she fully closes the other one.*

"Yeah, that is true. It's just…"

"Just what, dear?"

"I don't know, really. He's um… Sebastian is his name, but he's also going through a very difficult time in his life as well. He was supposed to get married, and his bride to be left him standing at the altar. I was at the wedding and saw it all. We weren't close then, but since that happened, we have gotten closer. I don't know though… Sebastian asked me whether I thought he would ever love again and I told him sure, with God's help, he would. He then told me that he doesn't believe in God. I believe that alone will alter our friendship," Satin shared with Karen. She trusted her input and wanted some feedback.

"Aw child, what are you talking about? You just told me that this guy was a good person basically. He cares about you, and has been helping you; despite his own troubles, get through your troubles. The man is not dead, or a lost cause, he's broken; his spirit is broken." *A man whose interested in marriage which is designed by God. That's a good sign.*

"Broken… Hmm… interesting. That is the exact term he used last night. But, how do I fall in love with a broken man? How do I even love one when he doesn't even know if he is capable of loving another woman again?"

Karen walked over to Satin. She gently placed her hand on Satin's shoulder.

"You know… sometimes the people who are the hardest to love turn out to be the ones who need it the most. You love a broken man the same way you love a man that's not broken. That's how you love one, it's simple. But hey, what do I know." Karen removed her hand from Satin's shoulder and went back to her seat and sip more coffee. "I'm just an old lady who has been where you're going, and who has lived where you have yet to begun," Karen continued as she winked.

Satin stood still and let everything Karen told her sank in. She inhaled and exhaled before speaking. "On that note, I'll go on and get ready for work. Thanks for listening, and thanks for always giving me a different perspective."

"Anytime. I'm here whenever you need more." Karen raised from her seat again and begun to get the oatmeal out of the pantry.

She sat it on the counter so it would be in reach when she was ready to start breakfast for Noah and Little Darrius. Karen looked in the refrigerator to make sure there was enough of the mixed fruit she made the day before so she could add it to the children's breakfast.

Satin walked out the kitchen, checked on Noah and then went home to dress for work.

Chapter Nineteen

Every Beginning Has an End

Satin arrived at work thirty minutes early. She had really been trying her damndest not to do anything that would give Janice ammunition to fire her, and she had succeeded thus far.

Satin walked into the break room and noticed a few of her colleagues in a huddle. When Satin walked in, everyone hushed, as if she was the topic of their conversation. Eyes begun to wander and mouths immediately shut. Some of them wondered how she captured Sebastian's attention when they all were basically throwing themselves at him. Satin quickly noticed the silence and the bleak stares. She placed her bowl into the microwave to warm the oatmeal, bacon and scrambled eggs Karen prepared for her. After her food was warmed, Satin removed the bowl from the container and sat at an empty table.

Three of the woman got up from their table and walked out. The other two finished their coffee and then walked out a few minutes later. Satin ended up in the break room alone and it was perfectly okay with her.

"What a way to clear a room. I wonder what that was all about," Satin said out loud as she took a spoon of her sweet oatmeal. Brandy walked into the break room and Satin smiled when she saw a friendly face.

"Good morning, babe. How are you this lovely morning?" Brandy asked as she walked straight to the brewing coffee pot, her early morning addiction.

"Hey B. I'm good, how are you?"

"Girl, I couldn't be any better. Lucky came over last night and I got to tell you he got me thinking about having his baby. Damn... that nigga put it all the way down."

Satin tittered. "Oh goodness, take it from me. Being some dude's baby momma ain't all what it's cracked up to be, but I'm glad you enjoyed your night."

"Yasss girl, I really did. But seriously, I think I really like him. He wants us to um... be in a relationship, and I told him I'll think about it and get back to him," Brandy stated as she grabbed her coffee and sat across the table from Satin.

"Girl, take your time. Do not rush something if you're not ready. You've been really thriving in your singlehood. Why the sudden change?"

Brandy reflected on Satin's question a minute before she answered. "I don't know. I guess the single life is not all what it's cracked up to be either. I really think I'm ready."

Satin just looked at Brandy. She wanted to share what had happened between her and Nolan, but wasn't sure if she could trust Brandy with her business, being as though Brandy was also friends with the same three ladies who stopped talking when she had walked into the break room. One of the things Satin didn't care much for was females who friendly bobbed with every other female. Brandy was that kind of female by default, but she had started to like Brandy.

"Well B, only you know when you're ready. I'll say, if you're ready for a serious relationship, go for it. I wish you all the best," Satin said as she thought about Sebastian and how she wanted to pursue a relationship with him, but knew that they both needed to heal from past hurt before getting seriously involved with each other.

"Thank you, I appreciate that. So, are you finally ready to be honest with me about you and ole boy?"

"Ole boy?"

"Oh, don't act like you don't know what I'm talking about."

"Nolan?"

"No, the other Nolan, and I'm not talking about your son Noah either."

Satin simply smiled. *He's very far from being anything like Nolan, believe me.* "I take it that you're talking about Sebastian?"

"Ding," Brandy made a sound of a bell as she sipped her coffee. Satin continued to smile. She never confessed her true feelings about Sebastian to Brandy, and never had any intention of ever doing so, but it was written all over Satin's smile when his name was mentioned, and Brandy was no fool.

"We're just friends, that's it, friends," she lied, and Brandy knew doggone well there was way more to Satin and Sebastian.

"So, let me ask you this?"

"I'm listening."

"How long are you going to parade around here like nothing more is going on between you and Sebastian? I don't know why you're trying to hide it. EVERYONE around here knows the two of you are indeed messing around. Girl, please."

"Well, I guess all of you know more than me then because from our mutual understanding, he and I are JUST FRIENDS," Satin said as she raised up from the chair and walked over to the sink. She rinsed her bowl out and placed it back inside her lunch bag. Satin opened one of the cabinets and placed her bag there until later that evening when she got off. Brandy just sat and kept quiet as she finished her coffee.

"I'll see you at the station," Satin said as she smiled at Brandy and walked out.

"Mmm hmm…" Brandy responded as she shook her head and laughed at herself at Satin trying to hide what was really going on with her and Sebastian.

*****

The doors of the bank had just opened for business and every employee was at their station and the white collars were in their offices. Las Vegas Metropolitan Police marched through the doors and hijacked everyone's attention without even asking for it. Every teller's eyes widened and they immediately stopped what they were doing. The bank hadn't filled with customers yet, and the police were outside waiting for the bank to open so they could ambush as soon as the lock unlashed.

Satin eyes instantly followed suit as she stood at the station. Brandy's facial expression told it all. She looked as if she had seen a ghost. "Girl, what the…," Brandy asked as she looked at Satin, and in a flash, drew her attention back to the police, who were filling the bank one by one. Satin hunched her shoulders because she didn't have a clue as to what was about to transpire. The boys in khaki walked through the bank as if they owned it, and their demeanor dared anyone to get in their way. The officers of the law passed by Satin and Brandy and headed straight for Sebastian's office.

Brandy gasped and put her hand over her mouth. She looked at Satin again. Satin kept her cool, but followed the officers every move towards Sebastian's office. Her eyes stayed planted on the officers. Three officials entered Sebastian's office, two stood on the outside the door as if they were guarding it. Janice got word from Rayanne that the officers were there, and so had Frank, Paul and Alex. Janice powerwalked to the doors and locked them back. She didn't want customers entering while the bank was filled with police officers. She then walked to the tellers' station and stood before them.

"Unfortunately, this morning, we have a situation that involves the police department. I will ask that you all remain calm, and stay confined to your stations until further notice. We must conduct ourselves as professionals at all times, and from my understanding, with the information that was given to me, everything is under control and will be handled properly. It will be over before you know it. The police are here for one reason and one reason only. It has nothing to do with any of you, so there's no need to panic or freak out. Once they leave, I will reopen the doors to the bank and we will carry on with business as usual. Do I make myself clear, and is there any questions?"

Everyone said no, but Satin just stared. Janice waited around for a second, but no one had questions and she walked off. Janice then walked towards Sebastian's office and joined Paul, Alex and Frank.

"Sebastian Smith, you are under arrest for the robbery of this bank, Bank of America," one officer said as the other walked behind the desk and ask Sebastian to stand. Sebastian stood in disbelief and was asked to place his hands behind his back.

"What the hell is going on here? Frank, you got to be kidding me, man. Really, y'all just gon' let this go down like this after everything that I've done for this bank? I didn't do it; I didn't do it!" Sebastian begin to raise his voice and the entire staff heard him from behind the walls of his office.

Satin's eyes were filled with worry; she couldn't believe what was taking place right before her very own eyes. Sebastian, the man who she had become very fond of was being detained by the police for allegedly robbing the bank. Everything Brandy had told her started to replay in her head. Satin couldn't believe that Brandy and the rest of Sebastian's accusers may have been right.

The officer continued to read Sebastian his Miranda rights. "You have the right to remain silent and refuse to answer questions. Anything you say can and will be used against you in a court of law. You have the right to speak to an attorney before speaking to the police and to have an attorney present during questioning now or in the future. If you cannot afford an attorney, one will be appointed for you before any questioning if you wish. If you decide to answer questions now without an attorney present, you will still have the right to stop answering at any time until you talk to an attorney. Knowing and understanding your rights as I have explained them to you, are you willing to answer any questions without an attorney present?"

"I understand completely, and no I will not be answering any questions without my attorney present," Sebastian answered with angry eyes, and tightened lips as he clenched his teeth. If Sebastian thought he could break away without getting shot and possibly killed, he would have beat the living shit out of Frank, Alex and Paul, who stood and didn't say a word. It was as if they knew the police were coming to arrest Sebastian that morning. Sebastian believed they were the ones who were responsible for his detaining.

"Okay, as you wish," the officer answered and looked over at Frank. "I apologize for any inconvenience that was caused here on our behalf this morning. We are done and you may now return to business."

Frank, Paul and Alex all nodded at the officer as he began to escort Sebastian out of the office, handcuffed with his hands behind his back. Sebastian knew, without a doubt, that Frank was the mastermind behind his arrest. He believed that Frank was the one who ultimately put the arrest in motion. He was the main one of the three who undermined Sebastian's spreadsheets all the time.

Sebastian was convinced that Frank was scared that he would replace him in the bank as the Portfolio Manager, who grossed over two hundred thousand a year, if given the opportunity. Sebastian did well as the bank's Tax Accountant IV and grossed over a hundred thousand himself and did well with his side hustle for small businesses as their personal accountant.

The arresting officer led Sebastian. Following behind him was an officer on each side of him and a couple behind him. Satin stood at the station and just could not believe what happened. When the officers approached the front of her station, Sebastian planted his feet and did not move. He looked over at Satin.

I didn't do this, Satin. I swear to you, I didn't do this, Sebastian pleaded with drooping eyelids that displayed his hurt and sorrow.

"Please keep it moving, Mr. Smith," the officer requested.

"Satin, take my wallet and keys. I'll call you once I'm booked," Sebastian suggested.

Satin immediately walked from behind her station and stood in front of Sebastian.

"Mr. Smith, I said keep it moving. You cannot remove anything at this time. You may have someone to come and pick up your property once booked," the officer instructed.

"Man, come on now, so you mean to tell me I can't give my girlfriend my valuables right now, and she's standing right here? I can't run, I'm handcuffed."

"Mr. Smith, you will need your identification once you get to the station for proper verification."

"Man, y'all know exactly who I am. You know where I work. You been investigating me for weeks now. You came straight in my office and called me by my full name. What more identification do you need? I need my girlfriend to get my property, please. I would really appreciate it. That's the least y'all can do after embarrassing me in front of my colleagues."

The lead detective nodded his head yes. "She cannot take anything out of your pocket, so if you need her to have it, I'll need to go in and give it to her. Is that okay, Mr. Smith?"

"Yes, sure. My wallet is in my left back pocket, and my keys are in my front right pocket," Sebastian spoke in gratitude. He didn't want to chance his personal belongings getting lost in the system.

The officer went in both pockets and got Sebastian's belongings. "Before I hand your keys over, I'll have to remove your vehicle key, and also your house key. It's evidence. Everything else your girlfriend can have."

Sebastian shook his head. "Yeah, okay."

The officer asked Sebastian what key belonged to what and he handed the rest to Satin. She accepted them and just stared at Sebastian, speechless. Everyone in the bank was quiet as a mouse. Bank of America had become The Sebastian and Satin Show.

"I'll call you," Sebastian spoke for the last time.

"Okay." Satin muttered under hear breath because she could barely speak.

"Girlfriend?" *This sneaky bitch been lying the entire time,* Brandy thought to herself.

The Las Vegas Metropolitan Police escorted Sebastian out of the bank. The newscasters were outside, waiting with flashing lights from the cameras. Sebastian held his head down as he was escorted into the back of a police car. When he arrived at the police station, he was put in a waiting cell. Sebastian's faith and freedom was in the hands of the District Attorney, and whether he would be charged for a crime he swore he did not commit.

TO BE CONTINUED....

How To Love A Broken Man 2

Will Be The Next Release By

Author MyKisha Mac

Be sure to text ANEWCHAPTER at 22828

to sign up for the mailing list to receive

a sneak peek for:

How To Love A Broken Man 2

and sneak peeks for up and coming books

Would you like to read a book FIRST, before it becomes available to the world?

If you're interested in being a TEST READER for A New Chapter reading group, join today! Click on link TODAY. >>

https://www.facebook.com/groups/anewchapter.mykishamacreaders/

ONLY

A New Chapter

members get a chance

to become test readers.

Have You Read Any Of

These Best Sellers

By: My Kisha Mac

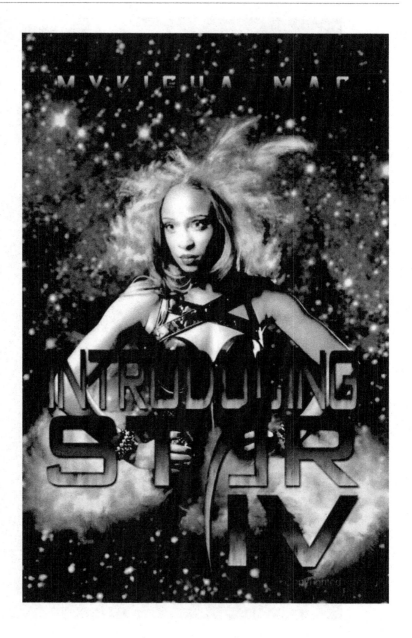

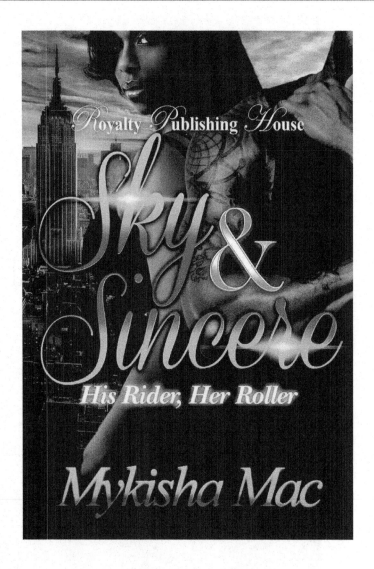

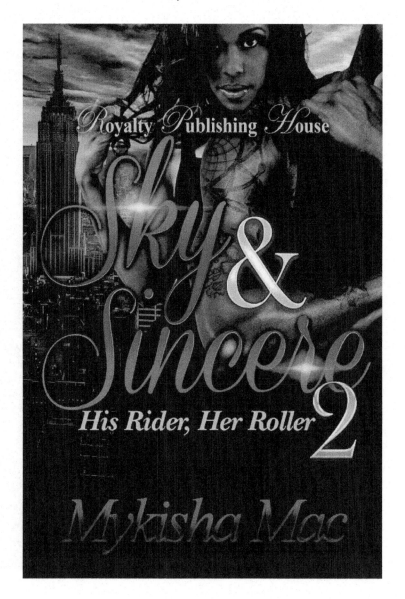

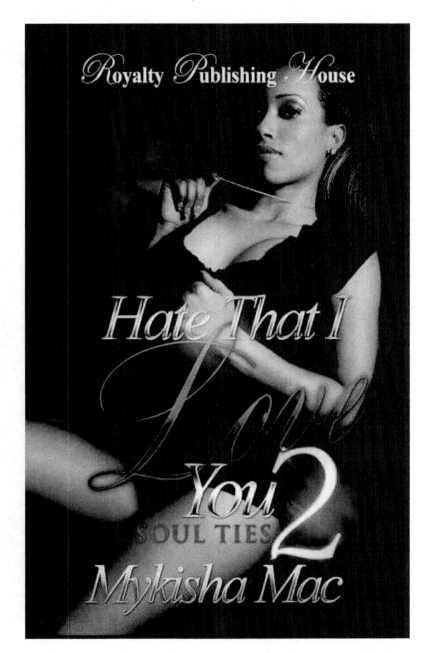

MyKisha Mac

CPSIA information can be obtained
at www.ICGtesting.com
Printed in the USA
LVOW13s1740270317

528626LV00011B/1382/P

9 781544 276465